# UNDERSTANDING **DREAMS**

# UNDERSTANDING DREAMS

PAUL ROLAND

hamlyn

First published in Great Britain in 1999 by
Hamlyn, a division of Octopus Publishing Group Ltd
2–4 Heron Quays, London E14 4JP

This revised edition published 2005

ISBN 0 600 61220 1
EAN 9780600612209

A CIP catalogue record for this book is available
from the British Library

Printed and bound in China

10 9 8 7 6 5 4 3 2 1

# CONTENTS

# INTRODUCTION

THE NOVELIST L. P. Hartley (1895–1972) once remarked 'the past is a foreign country; they do things differently there.' He might just as easily have been describing the often surreal world of dreams where most of us spend a third of our lives, but which some still consider to be as insignificant as a television soap opera.

Even if we awake from a nightmare that has seemed all too real, or a vivid dream teeming with what may be significant imagery, it is rare for us to reflect on it beyond breakfast, or make it more than the subject of an idle chat with friends.

And yet, our dreams are the sum of all that we have experienced and all that we have the potential to become. One problem is that, although we spend 25 years of the average lifetime dreaming, we rarely remember more than five per cent of our adventures. The dreams that we do manage to recall are often couched in such obscure or surreal symbolism that we dismiss them as fantasies.

This might stem from the fact that most of us live our lives so fast that we do not have the time to savour the sensations. Our experiences and emotions are compressed into fleeting impressions that are reflected in our dreams in forms we are unable to appreciate. We tend to view sleep as an interruption, and our dreams are considered to be analogous to the processing functions of a supercomputer.

Not all civilizations dismiss dreams so lightly, and not all cultures continue to ignore the possible hidden meanings. The Senoi, for example, a people living in the Malaysian rainforest, believe that the dreamworld is as real as the waking one and so everything they experience in their dreams has a purpose. For the Senoi the dreamworld is the world of spirit where the dreamer can face his fears and conquer them. Members of the tribe also practise transforming the negative actions of their dreams into positive actions in the real world in the belief that a function of dreams is to forewarn of the potential for conflict. Such techniques, together with similar practices utilized by indigenous peoples from Native Americans to Native Australians, are now being adopted by some dream therapists in the West. These people regard working with dreams as a valuable source of material for self-discovery and development. They make the point that the only way to transform the world is to first transform ourselves by listening to the inner voice of our dreams.

The sciences can play their part in this personal development, although so far study of sleep and dreams has generated a mass of knowledge but little understanding. After several centuries science is still no nearer to solving two of the fundamental mysteries of the human mind – the purpose of sleep and the function of dreams.

Psychoanalysis is also developing. It is less than a hundred years since the Austrian psychoanalyst Sigmund Freud (1856–1939) suggested that dreams express our secret repressed desires. But no matter how adarnantly we deny what drives, torments and inspires us, our dreams will find us out.

## UNDERSTANDING DREAMS

Although we may not remember our dreams when we wake up, we all dream on a nightly basis. Explanations for the phenomenon vary widely, from the divine inspiration credited to ancient pharaohs, prophets and seers, through the expression of our subconscious desires to our brains processing and filing the impressions of the day like a computer backing itself up.

Whichever of the many theories they subscribe to scientists, psychoanalysts and dreamworkers all acknowledge that our dreams are vital to our physical, mental and emotional wellbeing, although the precise mechanisms of how and why we dream are only now beginning to be understood.

# THE SCIENCE OF SLEEP AND DREAMS

SCIENCE has come a long way since the 'heavy supper' theories of the ancient Greeks to explain the physiological processes of the sleeping state. However, we are no nearer to understanding the necessity for sleep or the nature and purpose of our dreams than we were more than 2000 years ago. Science has identified, measured and analysed the biological and neurological processes involved and noted the traumatic effects of sleep deprivation, but has so far failed to explain the mysteries of the human mind.

## WHY DO WE SLEEP?

It is true that we have specific muscles that need periodic rest, but it is not biologically necessary for humans, or indeed most animals, to lapse into a regular and prolonged state of unconsciousness. Even chronic insomniacs succumb to at least a couple of hours' sleep every night. During the deepest stages of sleep – the stage in which the most vivid dreams occur – the sleeper is essentially unresponsive to stimuli and is extremely difficult to rouse. While this may be no more than an inconvenience to us today, it put our ancestors, as well as many animals, at considerable risk from predators.

So why do we sleep? What purpose does it serve and what happens if we resist the impulse to sleep?

The philosopher Aristotle (384–322 BC) proposed that sleep was a state of unconsciousness induced by 'internal evaporation' of undigested substances following a meal. Having a basic knowledge of anatomy and the digestive process, he assumed that these warm gases would rise to the head and anaesthetize the brain. 'This explains,' he said, 'why fits of drowsiness are apt to come on after meals; for the matter, both the liquid and the corporeal, which is born upwards in a mass, is then of considerable quantity.' He reasoned that after a certain time the gases cooled and descended to lower parts of the body, prompting the sleeper to awaken.

The speculations of Ivan Pavlov (1849–1936), the eminent Russian neurophysiologist, were almost as fanciful as those of Aristotle. His discovery of the conditional reflex in dogs led him to erroneously assume that the brain automatically shuts down when sensory input falls below a certain level. In other words, we sleep because our brains get bored.

Another popular myth is that sleep is the body's way method of conserving energy, a doctrine enthusiastically promoted by the American psychologist Frederick Snyder. Unfortunately, he failed to take into account the fact that if that is the only purpose sleep serves, we would be able to breed that mechanism out of any species we chose now that we can cater for an animal's every need.

## THE BRAIN DURING SLEEP

Most of us tend to think of sleep as being a serene, almost hibernetic-like state, but in fact, even the most peaceful sleeper moves every few minutes to keep the blood circulating through the limbs and to prevent stiffness in the muscles and joints. This contradicts the common assumption that we sleep to give our body, or brain, rest. Most of the critical muscular components of the body, such as the heart, do not need cyclic periods of 'rest'. Nor does the brain, which continues to work away during even the deepest phases of sleep with sustained bursts of activity that can exceed those of the waking state. In fact, electrical activity within the brain during the dreaming phase is so violent and sustained, in contrast to the limpness of the body, that researchers have concluded that it is as if the brain has become detached from the body.

Clearly, sleep serves a purpose, but even the most eminent scientists still do not fully understand what it is.

> ## 'we all intermittently experience insanity'
>
> Ian Oswald

## WHAT THE SCIENTISTS SAY

Orthodox science defines dreaming as a purely mental activity of electro-biological origin in which the brain processes our thoughts, memories and emotions in an apparently random and purposeless fashion.

Science sees the human brain from a purely physiological point of view, as a soft, convoluted mass of nervous tissue that controls and co-ordinates the nervous system, as well as our thoughts, memories and emotions. Thus the majority of our dreams may be viewed as a peripheral phenomenon and merely the result of a processing function of this biological supercomputer. This does not help to answer what dreams are or why we need to dream at all.

After making a life-long study of the phenomenon of sleep, specialist Ian Oswald, a Professor of Psychiatry at the University of Edinburgh, was forced to come to the conclusion that in sleep 'we all intermittently experience insanity'.

## BRAIN ACTIVITY

Part of the problem is that serious scientific investigation into dreams is still in its infancy. It began only relatively recently with the experiments of the German psychiatrist Hans Berger in the 1920s. Berger devised a method of measuring the electrical activity within the brain by wiring electrodes to the scalp. He then recorded the various frequency modulations with an instrument of his own devising, which he called an electroencephalograph (EEG). From the resulting data Berger discovered that there are characteristic patterns associated with different states of consciousness.

＊ Alpha waves are bursts of electrical activity from the cerebral cortex of a drowsy or inactive person which occur at a frequency of between 8 and 12 Hertz.

＊ Beta waves are electrical activity occurring in the higher range of 13 to 30 Hertz, which were indicative of an active person.
＊ Delta waves are the third and lowest frequency of detectable brainwaves, occurring at between 1 and 4 Hertz during periods of deep sleep.Other wave patterns were discovered later by other researchers.

In the 1950s American scientists Nathaniel Kleitman and his co-pioneers, Eugene Aserinsky and William Dement, utilized Berger's EEG machine for dream research. By observing and measuring the physiological fluctuations of their subjects, in particular their eye movements, parallel to the brainwave patterns they discovered that sleep can be divided into two categories.
＊ REM (rapid eye movement or paradoxical).
＊ NREM (non-rapid eye movement or orthodox sleep).

## THE NEED TO DREAM

Kleitman and his colleagues deduced that for every 100 minutes of sleep, we experience 70–90 minutes of NREM sleep before drifting into the deeper REM dream state for 10–20 minutes. The cycle repeats through the night, reflecting a similar cycle of day-dreaming at 90–100 minute intervals during waking hours.

Having woken and questioned volunteers about their dreams during both REM and NREM phases, Kleitman concluded that detailed descriptions would be elicited if a subject was awoken during REM sleep, while only sketchy impressions would be gleaned if a volunteer was awoken during the NREM phase. Moreover, if a volunteer was repeatedly awoken during the REM phase, he or she would later compensate for the interruptions by indulging in longer periods of REM sleep when allowed to sleep on. In essence, this research suggests that we need to dream.

## THE FIVE STAGES OF SLEEP

Sleep can be divided into five distinct stages, the first four of which are classed as Non-Rapid Eye Movement sleep. These are characterized by thoughts rather than dreams.

✳ In the first, the 'alpha' stage, so called because the brain is producing alpha brainwaves, the heart rate slows and the muscles relax.

✳ The second stage is characterized by brief bursts of short-wave brain pulses. These invariably lead to the large, slow brainwaves of stage three.

✳ Stage three sees a further drop in the heartbeat and falls in blood pressure and body temperature.

✳ The fourth stage is known as 'delta' sleep – the lower frequency delta waves are produced in this relaxed state when the body is immobile.

✳ The fifth, and final, stage sees the drift into the REM phase where our most vivid dreams occur. This phase is also called paradoxical because the brainwaves indicate alertness, the adrenal glands secrete adrenaline in preparation for action, the muscles twitch and yet the body is limp and oblivious to external stimuli.

## SLEEP DEPRIVATION

All attempts to tamper with the sleep function in both animals and humans have had disturbing results – sometimes these have been disastrous and occasionally even fatal.

Animals kept awake for more than four days invariably die from severe anaemia and hypothermia following behavioural disturbances ranging from restlessness and photophobia to eating disorders. In one series of experiments, rats were seen to become so irritable that they fought each other to the death. Human beings have a higher tolerance level, but depriving people of sleep for more than two weeks inevitably leads to madness and finally death.

## DREAM DEPRIVATION

Researchers conducting a series of monitored experiments at the University of Chicago found that depriving someone of the dream phase of sleep had worse consequences than merely depriving them of sleep. Subjects were allowed to sleep but were woken when they entered the REM phase. As if to compensate, the REM phases increased in number as the experiment progressed to a point where the volunteers sank into REM sleep immediately they were allowed to sleep. When they were finally allowed a full night's sleep, they spent nearly 30 per cent of the night dreaming as opposed to the usual 20 per cent. Volunteers reported memory loss, lack of concentration, fatigue and irritability for a number of days.

## Hallucinations

The idea that dreams may be nothing more than random hallucinations triggered by a brain deprived of sensory input is one that some scientists resort to when confronted by what they consider 'irrational' explanations offered by mystics and psychologists as to the true nature of dreams.

Certainly, this theory might account for some of the more abstract dreams, but it clearly fails to explain those dreams which have proven to be precognitive and the even greater number which have revealed insights into the psyche of the dreamer.

Hallucinations, or 'waking dreams', are a common feature of drug and alcohol abuse and withdrawal, some mental disorders and the transitional phase between sleep and waking. These are known as hypnagogic hallucinations. It could be argued that both dreams and hallucinations occur when the mechanism that censors, filters and sorts sensory input is disconnected, whether by the use of chemicals, biological malfunction or when the brain is drifting from the unconsciousness of sleep to the waking state. A clue to the nature of dreams might, therefore, be gleaned from looking at hallucinations, particularly those that can be induced when sensory deprivation occurs.

## Sensory Deprivation

The most radical experiments into the effects of sensory deprivation were carried out by the American military in the 1950s. These experiments were instigated after a number of American jet pilots reported having disturbing hallucinations at extreme high altitude where the vibration of the plane was negligible and the sky a featureless icy blue. In these situations pilots often became disorientated and their perceptions distorted. Several reported hallucinations similar to those experienced by people tripping on LSD, such as one pilot who spoke of seeing his limbs growing longer and longer and his body blending into the aircraft.

In the 1960s NASA scientists devised a series of 'sensory deprivation' studies in which volunteers were kitted out in astronauts' suits and suspended in a bath of warm water in an isolation tank with no sound or light to help them orientate themselves. Even hardened combat pilots demanded release from the tank within a few hours. All of the participants complained of being haunted by luridly coloured creatures, hideous faces, insects and uncanny, distressing sounds.

The scientists concluded that, deprived of sensory input, the brain substitutes stimuli from its own memory banks, stimuli which, being distorted and uncensored, are emotionally disturbing to the conscious mind. But this does not explain why the substitute stimuli from the subject's own memory banks should be of such a grotesque and horrific nature. Perhaps it is because isolated in the blackness the primitive instincts of the volunteer naturally prevail, namely fear of the dark or unknown, and therefore the 'visions' are of a primitive nature.

### THE SHADOW SELF

We make our own monsters in the realm of dreams. Jungians (see page 12) would call such a character 'a shadow' as it personifies aspects of our unconscious personality without which we are not truly 'whole'. C.G. Jung himself recorded several dream-encounters with his own shadow who once appeared as a handsome Arab prince. The prince attempted to drown Jung, but was eventually subdued. In this instance the struggle was seen as a symbol of Jung's attempt to suppress a part of his personality 'which had become invisible under the influence and pressures of being European'.

'The primitive psyche of man borders on the life of the animal soul, just as the caves of prehistoric times were usually inhabited by animals before men laid claim to them.'

C. G. Jung

## THE PSYCHOLOGY OF SLEEP

Psychoanalysis is a method of studying the human mind and the motivations behind our behaviour based on an exploration of the unconscious. Its most valuable source of material is our dreams, which reflect both our inner and outer life.

Contrary to Freud's belief (see box), our dreams are not exclusively comprised of wish-fulfilment fantasies. Nor are they merely surreal scenes randomly thrown together from memories. They may seem as complex, irrational and enigmatic as we are, but once we understand the language of dreams we have the key to the unconscious. In this language resides the sum of all that we are and all that we have the potential to become.

### Jung and the House of the Psyche

It is an apparent paradox of modern psychoanalysis that one of its principal concepts was revealed to its founder C. G. Jung (1875–1961), the Swiss psychologist and psychiatrist, in a dream.

Jung had experienced premonitory dreams and visions from early childhood and was determined to reconcile the mystic's sense of wonder with a rational analysis of inner space – the uncharted regions of the mind. It was his assertion that paranormal phenomena were manifestations of the subconscious, or superior man, struggling to be heard.

Jung found himself on the second floor of a two-storey house he did not recognize but which he knew to be his own. The second storey comprised a comfortable salon elegantly furnished in a rococo style, and although Jung felt at ease here he was restless to explore the ground floor, which he found to be sombre, with floors of bare brick and the furnishings almost medieval in character. He descended a stairwell which led down into a vaulted chamber that appeared to have been built in Roman times. Beneath one of the stone slabs he discovered narrow stone steps leading down to a cave cut into the rock. In the cave he discovered shards of bone and broken pottery which he concluded must have been the remains of a primitive culture. Then, just as he was about to examine two human skulls, he awoke.

'It was plain to me that the house represented a kind of image of the psyche,' he later wrote, 'that is to say of my then state of consciousness, with hitherto unconscious additions. Consciousness was represented by the salon. It had an inhabited atmosphere … The ground floor stood for the first level of the unconscious. The deeper I went in, the more alien and darker the scene became. In the cave, I discovered remains of a primitive culture, that is, the world of primitive man within myself – a world which can scarcely be reached or illuminated by consciousness. The primitive psyche of man borders on the life of the animal soul, just as the caves of prehistoric times were usually inhabited by animals before men laid claim to them.'

## Collective unconscious

From the images of his dream Jung evolved the concept of the 'collective unconscious' ('das kollektive Unbewusste'), a stratum of the psyche incorporating memories, instincts and experiences common to all humanity. These patterns, which are inherited, may manifest themselves as dreams or mystical visions often in the form of archetypes – primordial images representing absolutes in the human psyche. Identical archetypes are to be found in the mythology of every race and culture in the world.

'Take the unconscious in one of its handiest forms, say a spontaneous fantasy, a dream, an irrational mood … or something of the kind, and operate with it … observe its alterations

## SIGMUND FREUD'S LEGACY

In the 1890s, many of the tortured souls who came to the clinic of the Austrian psychiatrist Sigmund Freud (1856–1939), the founder of psychoanalysis, were convinced that their nightmares and neuroses were aberrations of either their spirit or their mind.

People had been conditioned by both Church and society to believe that it was their duty to subdue their 'animal passions'. So Freud's announcement that even 'normal' people were prey to irrational impulses originating in an unconscious region of their minds over which they appeared to have no control was greeted with almost universal self-righteous indignation.

Freud struggled to find a method of communicating with the unconscious. It was not until he considered the frequency with which his patients referred their problems back to their dreams that he was faced with the solution. Far from being 'the expression of a fragmentary activity of the brain' dreams are, in Freud's famous phrase, 'the royal road to the unconscious'.

Freud went on to state, 'there is no series of associations which cannot be adapted to the representation of sexual facts', indicating that almost all of our dreams have a sexual significance, because the unconscious consists exclusively of sexual desires. In Freud's view all dreams are wish-fulfilment fantasies representing unsatisfied sexual desires, most of which our mental censor, which he calls the preconscious, has repressed.

As psychoanalysis has developed it has become evident that a single symbol often represents more than one idea, experience or emotion. For an accurate analysis it is necessary to identify all of the experiences that the symbol represents and not just the one which fits in with the favoured theory of the analyst.

## THE DREAM JOURNEY

Californian growth psychologist and dreamwork specialist Strephon Kaplan-Williams has developed what he claims to be a radical but consistently effective system of therapy based on a blend of Jungian psychology and Senoi shamanic dreamwork. He calls the process the 'dream journey' and likens it to a form of mythical quest in which the adventure is more important for personal growth than the prize. Kaplan-Williams' states that the Self, the balancing and centralizing function of the psyche, whose aim is the integration of all aspects of our personality, uses image-making to convey the energy patterns of our inner states.

Kaplan-Williams says that to discover our true selves, we have to become habitually self-reflective and self-aware through developing a relationship with our dream ego, the image of ourselves that we project into our dreams. It is through the actions and reactions of this dream personality that we can discover who we really are. However, it is not enough to intellectualize, analyse and interpret our dreams, because by doing these things we present ourselves only with situations to resolve, not the resolution itself. If dreams are to have any substantial and lasting effect on our lives, we must actualize them.

Working on the inner life in this way will eventually reflect in the image we project to the outer world as we learn to experience life more fully.

objectively … follow the subsequent transformations …'. This was Jung's advice after a lifetime wrestling with the problem of how to explore the unconscious to test the validity of what our dreams reveal.

## The Waking Dream

He seized on the idea of forging a psychic link between the conscious and unconscious mind through the process of what he called 'active imagination', so that both aspects of the personality could be integrated. This, he believed, was the only reliable means by which we can probe the depths of the unconscious in the waking state. In this technique, which is now the basis of the vast majority of dreamwork in the West, the practitioner is encouraged to mine the unconscious for material by drifting into a 'waking dream' whose images are to be regarded objectively.

## Gestalt

As much as we might like to think of ourselves as rational, integrated human beings our dreams occasionally reveal what appear to be unpleasant facets of our personality of which we were blissfully unaware. And yet, how can we be certain that these aspects are really part of our psyche and not merely fantasy figures from the subconscious?

One of the most dramatic techniques which both professional and amateur analysts can utilize in their work is derived from a branch of psychotherapy known as Gestalt. The aim of Gestalt, which was devised in the 1950s by a psychiatrist called Fritz Perls, is the integration of the various, often contradictory, aspects of the personality so that patients can once again become 'themselves' as fully as possible, rather than become what they believe they ought to be. It is a process that requires them to reclaim aspects of their

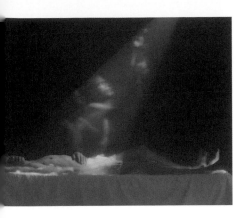

In our more secular and, perhaps, more enlightened age we are beginning to accept the possibility that anyone and everyone can explore the uncharted regions of the dreamscape at will in search of creative inspiration, visions of the future and, ultimately, glimpses of a greater reality.

## Great Dreams – Glimpses of a Greater Reality

Dreams of revelation, or 'great dreams', as Jung called them, are not the exclusive preserve of ancient kings, saints, visionaries or biblical prophets. Anyone and everyone can experience these glimpses of a greater reality regardless of their religious beliefs or their way of life.

The people who have revelatory dreams are invariably touched and transformed by a sense of something that they are later at a loss to describe, for it is an impression of something beyond human understanding.

Such dreams can occur at any moment, not necessarily at times of crisis. They do, however, often happen when the dreamer has been struggling in their waking life (even subconsciously) to find the meaning and purpose of existence. The irony is that it is only when the mental struggle ceases and the rational mind is at rest that these revelations overwhelm us. Great dreams are always an intense and memorable experience, and they always change the dreamer's life profoundly.

## Dreams of Prophecy and Prediction

One of the most fascinating aspects of precognition – the ability to foresee the future in visions and dreams – is not the fact that such a phenomenon exists, but the extent of these experiences among 'ordinary' people. This suggests that precognition is a 'lost' sixth sense that we all share.

personality they have disowned, and without which they cannot in effect be complete as a person.

In adapting the technique for dreamwork (see pages 21–29), each character who appears in the dream should be seen by the dreamer as an aspect of our own personality, which we are unconsciously struggling to integrate in order to make ourselves 'whole' again. This involves the dreamer acting out each character's part in turn so that he or she can appreciate the various points of view and thereby reveal the 'hidden message' the dream is trying to convey.

## DREAMS – THE UNCHARTED COUNTRY

Our ancestors in ancient times believed that meaningful dreams were of supernatural origin and were the exclusive preserve of prophets and kings. The main purpose of these dreams was to forecast the fortunes of rulers and their enemies. With the establishment of orthodox religion came a new idea: that the dreams of prophecy and revelation came by grace from God to His chosen vessels and consisted almost entirely of warnings not to stray from the moral teachings laid down by His self-appointed mediators – the priesthood.

## Johanna Bravand

In April 1960 Swiss hotelier Frau Johanna Bravand dreamed of a female corpse, wearing one of her own dresses, floating in a drinking trough. Johanna was certain that the body had been that of her sister Mina. In a second dream she was being chased by an unseen pursuer across a bridge over a river. Looking to her left and right, she saw two other bridges.

Some days later news reached her that Mina had gone missing. Johanna set off to search for her and ended up at their birthplace, Gotisberg. There, she came upon the three bridges.

She turned to a dowser with a reputation for tracing missing persons, who informed her that Mina had died by drowning, was held down by a piece of metal and told her where to find the body. When Johanna went to identify her sister's body, it had been placed in a metal-lined coffin, which Johanna had mistaken for a drinking trough in her dream, and it was wearing one of her own dresses.

Many of our nightly dreams may have a precognitive element, when the rational mind is sleeping and the latent psychic faculties are unhindered by the intellect, but unless they are highlighted by an emotional charge we tend to forget them on awakening.

### Doctor Dream's Journal

The possibility that we all dream of future events but do not recognize them as such was first proposed in the 1930s by mathematician John William Dunne (1875–1949).

Dunne called the phenomenon 'dreaming true' and in his international best-selling book *An Experiment With Time* he urged his readers to keep a dream journal so that they could prove to themselves whether their dreams were truly precognitive.

Dunne believed that most of us fail to identify these dreams as fleeting glimpses into the future because we are confused by the surreal imagery of the subconscious which obscures their real significance. The problem is that dream imagery is largely symbolic and composed of distorted fragments, which makes any interpretation highly subjective.

However, he argued that the significance of the imagery will eventually become clear if we record the details upon waking. As an example he cited a dream in which a man had burning cigarettes thrown at his face by an angry mob. Some days later the man was working with a circular saw when it struck a nail, showering him with sparks.

## DREAMING OF DISASTER

The most curious aspect of the phenomenon is the fact that the majority of events which Dunne's readers recorded, and which they considered to be precognitive, were often routine and of little significance even to themselves. To explain the phenomenon Dunne formulated a theory that all human beings exist at various levels of consciousness simultaneously, but that most of the time our least perceptive self, the observer, dominates, cruising on automatic pilot through the mundane activities of life. When we raise our awareness of the world through concentration, we shift into Self number 2, the selector. In sleep or meditative states a third, detached Self is allowed to drift free of the physical plane to perceive events in the future.

## DREAMS OF INSPIRATION

Many writers and artists have sought inspiration from their dreams although more often it was their nightmares which produced the most memorable creations.

Horace Walpole (1717–1797), the originator of the Gothic horror novel, used to eat raw meat before going to sleep in the belief that it would bring on the nightmares he needed as inspiration for his macabre tales. Mary Shelley (1797–1851), after being thrilled to the marrow by an evening of lurid ghost stories, was haunted by the nightmare that gave birth to her classic horror novel, *Frankenstein*. Other writers, such as Samuel Taylor Coleridge (1772–1834) and Thomas De Quincey (1785–1859), attributed their inspiration to dreams that they experienced under the effects of opium.

Romantic poets and authors of imaginative fantasy fiction tend to draw more inspiration from their dreams than mainstream fiction writers. The writer's darker fantasies are said to compensate for repressing the anti-social aspects of their personalities, while their heroic imaginings reflect a wish to overcome the dull routine of waking life.

The novelist Robert Louis Stevenson (1850–1894) recognized both his heroic and his shadow self in his tale *The Strange Case of Dr Jekyll and Mr Hyde*, the germ of which came to him in a dream. Stevenson had developed the art of what we now call creative dreaming, or dream incubation, in an effort to find inspiration for stories. He would begin a tale in his mind as he lay in bed, trusting in his 'brownies' (helpful night elves) to bring it to life in his dreams.

## Dreams and Demons

In a dark corner of one of London's leading occult bookshops stands a rack of bizarre prints depicting grotesque insect-like beings that might invade a naturalist's nightmare. Whenever a customer shows interest in the display the owner delights in telling him that such hideous beings are not figments of the anonymous artist's imagination, but elemental spirits he encountered on the astral plane. The fact that these eldritch horrors bear such a

### WARTIME DREAMS

A number of prophetic dreams have been experienced during wartime, a period when the anxiety and intensity of living with the prospect of sudden death appears to stimulate the latent psychic faculties of people who might otherwise scoff at the idea. Such experiences also emphasize the existence of what appears to be a subtle psychic link between close family members.

There are innumerable cases of parents experiencing precognitive dreams of their son's death in battle. Sometimes these dreams occur while the son is still a baby and invariably it is the mother who has the dream, no doubt because the emotional link is stronger due to the psychic bond formed in the womb and during the child's formative years.

'The most merciful thing in the world, I think, is the inability of the human mind to correlate all its contents.'

H.P. Lovecraft

## Neuroses and imagination

Although he proclaimed himself a rationalist and professed disbelief in the supernatural, Lovecraft was, it seems, both awed and terrified by the dark vistas of the inner eye, the surreal landscape and the inhabitants of those lower levels of consciousness which haunted him. His warnings of dabbling in these dark regions were encoded in stories whose recurrent theme was that of an elder race of malevolent, primal gods cast out of our world for practising black magic and now dwelling in a sixth dimension, 'not in the spaces known to us but between them … ever ready to take possession of this earth again.'

Perhaps he did not recognize, or did not wish to acknowledge, the true source of his inspiration. It might be that in indulging his fantasies in a vain attempt to escape the responsibilities and challenges of life, Lovecraft freed the inner demons of his subconscious – the fears, guilty feelings and anxieties given form by his overactive imagination.

Although Lovecraft maintained that he had no interest or knowledge of the supernatural, his stories describe a nightmare realm which is strikingly similar to ethereal worlds which the notorious magician Aleister Crowley (1875–1947) claimed to have explored through his psychic senses.

It is as if both Lovecraft and Crowley had tapped into what Jung called the 'collective unconscious', only Lovecraft tore the veil involuntarily during sleep while Crowley altered his perception at will.

striking resemblance to the hideous entities described by the American pulp horror writer H. P. Lovecraft (1890–1937) is due, we are to understand, to the fact that Lovecraft had also encountered them during out-of-body experiences. Lovecraft regularly dismissed these horrors as mere demons of his dreams, but he had to, because he had a fear of being overpowered by the creations of his own imagination, of being driven insane by them and of dying in a lunatic asylum like his father.

And yet, artists and writers are said to possess acute psychic insights as a consequence of honing their imagination and stimulating the extrasensory areas of the brain – a latent faculty the mass of humanity might have 'lost' because of its preoccupation with the concerns of the material world and what it perceives to be 'reality'.

> '...the most informative book you will ever read about dreams is the one you write yourself.'
>
> Hugh Lynn

# THE
# DREAMWORKER

DREAMWORK requires us to live our dreams rather than, as in dream interpretation, simply rationalize what they might mean. Our dreams are personal and often unique experiences which do not always conveniently conform to a particular school of analysis. Frequently, too, our dreams present only the problem and not the answer. We need simple, proven techniques to help us understand, identify and integrate the different aspects of our personality that they represent.

Dreamworking, in all its forms, offers the means through which we can develop a link between the conscious and unconscious mind so that we can use our dreams as a source of self-discovery.

In one important respect dreamwork is different from other techniques which aim to develop self-awareness, and that is that the following exercises and techniques require commitment and regular practice to bring results.

## DREAM DIARIES

One of the most perceptive comments on the subject of dreams was that made by Hugh Lynn, son of the legendary American sleeping prophet, Edgar Cayce (1877–1945), who said that the most informative book that you will ever read about dreams is the one which you write yourself.

Lynn was suggesting that anyone interested in dream analysis should keep a journal by their bed for recording as many details of their dreams as they can. Committing yourself in this way will send a message to the unconscious that its communications will be heeded. This in turn will strengthen the link between your sleeping and waking selves which will aid recall and can later be used for influencing the content of your dreams.

### TIP

For the visualizations and exercises in this section, read the scripts into a tape recorder, pausing when appropriate so that when you play the tape back your subconscious has time to absorb the suggestions. You can add some background music or natural sounds if you feel it will help you to relax and visualize the images. Allow the images to arise spontaneously and resist the temptation to analyse the details; just observe with quiet detachment. The house mentioned in the Dreamhouse of the Psyche exercise (see pages 24–25) symbolizes your psyche. As in all of these exercises, it could be beneficial to make a note of any impressions gleaned from the visualization for later analysis.

As well as helping to clarify any underlying problems in your life, a dream diary can also identify your deepest desires, anxieties and patterns of behaviour which may not be obvious during the day. You may also be surprised to discover the frequency with which the same themes recur, or that what appears to be an isolated scene is actually another episode in an on-going story screened in your mind on subsequent nights. This phenomenon is not as rare as you might think, but you probably will not be aware that it has happened to you unless you make an effort to record your dreams over a prolonged period.

Keeping a diary on a regular basis should also help to increase your ability to remember your dreams in more detail. So, the more you write each morning, the more you will remember of subsequent dreams. The more details you have, the more accurate your analysis will be.

### Keeping the Diary

* Each night before you go to sleep, aid your memory by 'programming' yourself to remember as many details as you can.
* Do this by imagining yourself waking up the next morning, recalling the images and detailing them in your diary.
* Tell yourself that you want to remember your dreams and that therefore you will remember them.
* Still your thoughts by imagining a pastoral scene or waves lapping upon a tranquil beach, and relax.
* Whenever you wake up, do not rush to write everything down. Wake up slowly, keeping your eyes closed, and try to remember as many details as possible. Bringing them piece by piece to the conscious mind in this way should draw out more than you can immediately recall and it will help fix them there.

* The overall atmosphere of the dream can be the key to its meaning, but it is also usually the first element to fade on waking, so make sure you note how you felt, as well as the storyline, symbols and incidental details. Do not dismiss any snippets of conversation which you heard yourself or the other characters in the dream saying, as these may hold vital clues. Resist the temptation to analyse the images until later.

* Finally, think back to any incidents or images during the previous week or so which may be inspirations for the dream while they are fresh in your mind and write them down.

## SERIAL DREAMS

These dreams, which tell a story in what appear to be unrelated episodes, are not uncommon. Most of us experience them from time to time, but do not recognize them for what they are.

A typical example was recorded by Dr J. A. Hadfield, an expert in psychoneuroses. Hadfield described a series of three dreams experienced by a patient during a single night. In the first the man travelled through a valley overhung with low, threatening clouds. In the second he entered an army cafeteria where he tried to get a table to himself, but the other officers refused to let him have it. In the third dream he had a fight with a lifelong friend ending with him knocking the friend unconscious.

Hadfield believed that the first dream presented the problem, that the man was suffering from depression, and the subsequent dreams identified the cause and suggested a solution. The struggle over the table hinted at the patient's selfish, anti-social nature and the fight symbolized the fact that the patient subconsciously identified his neurosis with his similarly selfish friend. Knocking out his friend was symbolic of the struggle he must have with his own arrogance.

## DREAMHOUSE OF THE PSYCHE VISUALIZATION EXERCISE

This is an exercise designed to give you an insight into your psychological state as it is at the moment.

## Script for visualization

**1** Close your eyes and imagine that you are returning to visit a house that you built many years ago, but which you have not visited for some time.

**2** As it comes into view, what is your initial impression? What are its surroundings like? What type of building is it? Note its size, style and as many exterior details as you can.

**3** Has it been well cared for or has it been neglected? Take a close look at the door where you will find your name. How is it inscribed?

**4** You open the door and enter the hallway. Take a few moments to consider the decor. Is it modern or old fashioned? What condition is the hallway in?

**5** Leave the hallway and enter the study. Is it tidy and well organized? Is your desk clear or piled with things that need attention?

**6** You find a sealed envelope which is addressed to you and has been lying there since your last visit. Open it and read the letter inside. What does it say?

**7** Leave the study, cross the hall and enter your studio. What is it that you do here when you have time for self-expression? Do you practise an art or craft or a discipline such as Yoga? Spend some time here doing one of these things while observing your reactions and your general attitude to the activity.

**8** Leaving the workshop you return to the hall and go to the basement. Here you will find the kitchen. How would you describe it? Are the stores well stocked? What type of food do you find on the table, if any?

**9** Leave the kitchen and locate the cellar where you check the boiler, water, gas and electricity. Are they working efficiently? Inspect the bathroom and toilet. Are they properly maintained? (The basement reveals the state of your health – so note the details carefully for later analysis.)

**10** Climb the stairs and return to the hallway, making your way to the rear of the house where you find the lounge. This is a room for relaxation where you are truly free to express your feelings. What are your impressions of the room?

**11** When you are ready, leave the house and go out into the garden. What season of the year is it and how does this season make you feel? Take a hard look at it. Is the garden large or small, a wilderness or well tended, formal or informal? Is it open or enclosed?

**12** You catch sight of an animal, your pet. What kind of creature is it? What does it tell you about your animal nature?

**13** You return to the house and climb the stairs to the first-floor dining room which is laid for a meal. Again take in the details and the decor. Are any changes needed to the room? Picture the guests you are expecting. Who are they? (This room and situation are a reflection of your social attitudes, your self-image and status as you imagine it to be at the present time.)

**14** Now leave the dining room and go to the upper floor of your house, where you will find a private attic room. Enter it and close the door behind you. This is where you keep your personal photographs, childhood treasures and mementoes. Beside these there is a diary in which you have recorded the major events of your life and also your most intimate thoughts and feelings. You flip through the pages and consider carefully what you find written there. When you have finished, looking up from the diary you notice a mirror on the wall and gazing into it you see yourself as you were when you were a child, then as a teenager and, finally, your face as you are now. What do these features say about you? What in that face do you hide from other people? What can others see that you had not realized they could see?

**15** When you are ready, leave the attic, closing the door gently behind you. Return to the ground floor, cross the hall and go into the study. Sit down by the desk and take out the letter. It might concern an important aspect of your life, an unresolved issue which you have been delaying dealing with, or a response to a matter concerning someone you know. Now is the time for you to write a reply. Place your answer in the envelope and take it with you to post. Your visit is now complete. Return to the hallway and take one last look round to get a sense of the entire house. Is there anything else you need to deal with before you leave? When you feel that you are ready to go, open the front door of the house and return to the outside world.

**16** As you leave the house, look back and take with you a final, overall, impression. What is it?

**17** Walk away from your dreamhouse, taking the occasional backward glance until you can no longer see the building.

**18** Open your eyes.

## A DREAMQUEST

To use your dreams to gain further insights into your psyche, try practising this exercise before going to sleep. A dreamquest can also be used to access a state of consciousness comparable to the dreamworld at any time of the day.

## Script for a dreamquest

**1** Imagine that you are at home preparing to set out on a quest. Take an inventory of your pack, maps and equipment. Do you really need these, or will you trust your intuition to take you safely to your destination?

**2** When you are ready, leave your home and walk through the familiar streets until you find a turning that you had not noticed before. It is an ancient path barred by a small gate, but you find that the gate is unlocked and swings open invitingly.

**3** Once you are through the gate the path leads you across unfamiliar terrain to a wood. What type of terrain is it and what are your feelings about entering the wood? Are you apprehensive or eager to explore? You enter the wood and follow a winding path through the undergrowth. Shortly you come to a clearing. There is something other worldly about this place, but you feel content and secure here. In the centre of the clearing you find a small pool of crystal-clear water. You stoop down and gaze into it. What do you see in the water?

**4** You take a short rest and on awakening you find that a change of clothes has been left for you. What does the choice of clothes tell you about yourself? You also discover that a horse has been left to take you on your journey. What type of horse is it and what does it tell you about your inner state? Mount the horse and ride, noting the type of terrain, until you come to a valley.

**5** Here you find a town which reflects the nature of your conscious mind. Observe all you can about its character, its condition and its citizens. Dismounting from your horse you walk the streets until you come to an inn. This symbolizes your ego. You enter, taking in as many details as you can about the decor, the state of the place and the customers. You pay particular attention to the innkeeper who comes over to serve you supper. You listen intently as he tells you the history of the town.

**6** On collecting your horse you find a gift has been left for you. What is it and what is its significance? If you do not know its significance, do not delay your journey. The answer will come to you later.

**7** You ride away from the town reflecting on what you have seen there.

**8** Eventually you come to a coastline. From the cliffs you can see an island far out to sea upon which can be glimpsed the faint outline of what appears to be a city. Then the sun is obscured by clouds and the vision vanishes into the horizon. You ride down to the shore by way of a gently sloping path.

**9** Once on the beach you are surprised to find a boat moored and waiting for you. You are even more surprised to discover that it has your name on the side. You dismount, tether the horse to a heavy piece of driftwood and examine the boat. Is it large or small? In good

condition or in disrepair? Is it suitable to take you on the final stage of your journey? Perhaps it has a crew and a captain. If so, what are they like? You climb aboard and set sail. The sky is clear and studded with stars, but a dense mist slowly closes in upon you. Moments later a sudden and unexpected storm erupts, causing a violent swell which tosses the boat from side to side. What is your reaction? Are you fearful or do you relish witnessing the forces of nature unleashed?

**10** Eventually the storm abates, the wind goes down, the waves subside and the mist surrounds you once again.

**11** Then the sun breaks through the clouds and reveals that you are approaching a port. Behind it rises a magnificent city. You dock at the harbour and follow a track to the gates of the city where two imposing guards look you over before allowing you to enter.

**12** You walk through the streets which become gradually narrower and quieter until you come upon a courtyard garden which appears to be a form of living museum stocked with objects reflecting the achievements, but also the negative aspects, of human history. You sit here for a moment and contemplate the exhibits. What insights do you receive?

**13** Looking up you notice what appears to be a small sanctuary half hidden from view. You approach it, the door opens and you enter to find yourself in a vast astronomical observatory, a place which you sense is beyond time and space.

**14** The walls are of crystalline light pulsing with the creative force of the universe. In the centre is a crystal covered with a dark cloth. You cross to it and find a card with your name on it which invites you to gaze into the crystal. With great care you remove the cloth. Do you ask a specific question or do you simply gaze into it? What do you hear or see?

**16** After looking into the crystal ball for what seems like an eternity, but is in fact only a few moments, a firm but kindly voice calls out your name and you are requested to leave the building so that the next traveller can enter. You replace the cloth over the crystal and retrace your steps out of the sanctuary, through the inner and outer courts, through the city gates and back to the port where your boat is waiting to take you back.

**17** You set sail and enjoy a peaceful return passage. At the far shore you disembark, mount your horse and set off for home, reflecting on your journey and experiences.

**18** When you are ready, return to waking consciousness and open your eyes.

## THE DREAMPOWER TAROT

In the introduction to his book *The Dreampower Tarot*, R. J. Stewart observes that the cards are a window into other worlds where the five regular senses are enhanced by the awakening of other subtle senses and energies. One world to which this particular deck of cards offers access is the world of dreams.

### Inner explorations

This world is considered to be sealed off from the conscious mind, but only because we assume it to be so. Practitioners of the tarot argue that dreams are confined to the sleeping state because that is the only time our preconscious is switched off for a significant length of time. We also put this censor into neutral when we daydream, but that is usually for just a few moments, allowing access only to thoughts just below the surface of consciousness.

Practitioners claim that using the 'Dreampower Tarot' in a deeper meditative state can help still our habitually fleeting thoughts and focus the subtle senses on inner visions, allowing access to the realm beyond sleep.

Stewart claims that the concept came to him spontaneously in what he describes as a 'waking vision'. In this altered state he 'saw' its inherent holism in the form of an inverted tree. So, rather than use the traditional Tree of Life which stretches up from earth to heaven and gives insights into the attributes of the Universal Creative Force, he generated the imagery of the Dreampower cards from a different pattern, one which has its roots in the outer world, but grows downwards, penetrating the Underworld, the primal reality out of which our surface world is reflected. In other words, the cards act as a prism for reflecting the myriad lights of a greater reality within ourselves, the body of the planet in which we are grounded and the beings which dwell there.

The magic of this particular tarot pack, according to Stewart, is that the beings in it will 'come alive' and communicate with the practitioner in dreams, visions, intuitions and 'exchanges of energy'. It is unimportant whether the forms in the cards are 'real' or not, he says, only that they embody certain changes in consciousness for the reader.

Stewart is convinced that this melding of tarot with dreamwork is only the beginning of a 'new expression of the tradition'. The value of such a deck is of course subjective, but an indication of the effectiveness of the symbolism for giving access to the dream realm may be gleaned from Stewart's assertion that various students with whom he was working prior to the pack's publication claimed to have visions of specific trumps with no prompting from him, and without any prior knowledge that he was working on such a project.

## LUCID DREAMING – CREATING YOUR OWN DREAMS

Lucid dreaming is apparently a common phenomenon in which at some point during sleep we become aware that we are dreaming and then go on to alter the imagery of our dream. It is common to everyone, though few recall it on waking and fewer still accept it for what it is. This is because subsequent dreams tend to obscure its significance, and also because it is the nature of the ego to deny everything greater than itself.

These dreams most frequently occur when the ego is at rest and the physical body is in such a deep state of relaxation that it allows the dream body (also known as the astral, etheric, subtle or emotional body) to temporarily drift free of its shell. In this heightened state we become aware of the astral world, which is a non-physical level of existence where energy vibrates at a higher rate or frequency than in our denser world of form and matter. It exists at the same frequency as our dream body and appears to radiate a clarity and intensity lacking in our physical world.

Habitual lucid dreamers, who make a practice of inducing the state, often report hearing 'wise inner voices' which chip in with profound insights to benefit their waking lives. They also claim that as they become more familiar with their elastic-like environment, they develop a greater ability to manipulate it.

To experience lucid dreaming for yourself, try the following self-hypnosis technique. If possible, listen to the tape on headphones as it will help you to absorb the suggestions at the subconscious level more effectively. The more often you do this exercise, the more control you will have over the content of your dreams.

## Script for self-hypnosis

1 Close your eyes and allow yourself to relax. Let all concerns fade away as you breathe slowly and deeply.

2 As you listen to these sounds and this voice you are drifting deeper and deeper into your own inner world where all your dreams are pleasant, where you can find peace and the solutions to any problems. Here, you, and you alone, are in complete control.

3 Let go and drift deeper and deeper with the passing of every word. Don't worry if you drift off to sleep – this voice will travel with you so that you will continue to respond to it at an unconscious level.

4 You are going to drift into a long, deep, refreshing sleep and when you awake you will be revitalized, invigorated and alert with all your cares washed away and replaced by a wonderful sense of wellbeing. There is nothing for you to do but relax … relax.

5 Now, imagine that you are standing on the terrace of a lovely old house, a country mansion or a cottage perhaps. You can feel the sun on your face and shoulders and a gentle breeze bringing the scent of freshly cut grass and summer flowers.

6 Looking around you notice an elegant flight of steps leading down into a sunken garden. There are ten steps and in a moment we will count down from ten to one together. As we count, imagine that each number is a step down towards this beautiful garden, another step down into an even deeper level of relaxation.

7 10 … take the first step down. Relax and let go … 9 … feel more and more relaxed … 8 … no need to hurry. Take your time … 7 … deeper and deeper … 6 … deeper and deeper still … 5 …really relaxed now. Letting go … 4 … becoming calmer and calmer … 3 … feeling safe and secure … 2 … all the way down now to …1.

**8** And now you find yourself in the beautiful garden with borders of sweet-scented flowers and lines of tall, elegant trees stretching far into the distance. Feel the softness of the freshly cut grass beneath your feet and smell the fresh, pure air. Listen to the birds singing as you absorb the stillness and serenity. In the distance you can see an ornamental fountain which is bubbling over into a gently trickling stream. You walk towards it and when you reach it you sit on the soft grass and gaze into the cool, clear water. The sound of the trickling water is lulling you to sleep so you lie back on the grass and gaze up at the clear blue sky. As you drift off into a deep sleep, you have a dream, a lucid dream in which you can control the events and maybe even find the answer to a question for which you have been searching. (Leave a long pause.)

In future, when you sleep, you will be able to take full control of your dreams, just as you are doing now. From the moment when your unconscious mind realizes that the events you are viewing are only part of a dream, you will say to yourself that this is a lucid dream and you will become aware of the limitless possibilities it offers for problem solving and self-exploration. Whenever this happens, you will be in full control at all times. You will be able to do anything you want and go anywhere you please and to awaken when you choose. You will only ever have pleasant, uplifting dreams. If you choose to find the solution to a problem for which you have been seeking an answer, you only have to step into that problem to find the solution. Your unconscious mind will guide you so that you can evaluate and try out as many of the solutions as are necessary. When you find the answer that both your conscious and unconscious minds believe is the best solution, you will feel completely satisfied and drift into a deep, comforting sleep. When you awaken in the morning you will have a full recollection of that solution.

From now on you will look forward to going to sleep as you will find it easy to recognize your dreams and become fully lucid whenever you want. You will find solutions to any problems, giving you more control of so many aspects of your life and making you feel more positive and optimistic for the future. Now go into a deep, deep sleep ....

Now you can discover what your dreams are trying to tell you!

# DIRECTORY

# OF DREAMS

**FEW OF US** experience Jung's 'Great' dreams and fewer still are haunted by precognitive dreams which appear to foretell future events. Most of us suspect our dreams reflect our day-to-day activities and anxieties. And yet, we all have our share of puzzling dreams and disturbing nightmares which seem to suggest the potential for problem-solving and personal development. But which of your dreams are significant and how can you discover just what they are trying to tell you? The following section comprises a comprehensive listing of about 250 dreams, the common themes and their meanings.

# Activity

IN OUR DREAMS we often find ourselves engaging in activities that we would never consider undertaking in waking life. By doing so, we are expressing our deepest emotions and exploring our secret hopes and fears within the safety of sleep.

The games we dream of playing with other people can reveal our attitudes towards authority, our sense of self-esteem and our true feelings for the other participants, but such dreams may also surprise us with insights into what other people think of us.

In the dreamscape we can explore the darkest recesses of our own psyche in search of a forgotten memory or something which will make sense of our present situation, and on rare occasions we may use our dreams to exorcise guilt by imagining ourselves accused of crimes which put our own minor failings and mistakes into perspective.

We may even find ourselves fleeing from imagined pursuers who are revealed to be our own shadows, or find ourselves enjoying the freedom of flight that seems so real that the border between sleep and other states of consciousness becomes blurred.

## FALLING

The sensation of falling may be caused by biological changes during sleep, such as a sudden fall in blood pressure or an involuntary muscle twitch called a myoclonic spasm. Often, though, it indicates the detachment of the dreambody from the physical. If you experience only the imagery and not the sensation of falling the dream may indicate a fear of failure. This type of dream is particularly common among the career conscious and the financially insecure, although it can also occur in the dreams of those who fear for the security of their relationships.

## RUNNING

Running towards someone, typically a partner or parent, without making any headway as they walk away indicates a fear of rejection or loss. This dream is particularly common among insecure and imaginative children whose parents are the main focus of their lives. If the dreamer is being chased, it usually indicates that a problem which has been suppressed into the subconscious is struggling to surface and demanding to be faced.

## ESCAPING

Dreams involving escape usually conclude a series of dreams in which the dreamer has felt trapped. Finding a way out or evading a pursuer indicates a positive end to a difficult period.

It might be valuable to use the Gestalt technique (described on pages 16–17) to adopt the personality of the pursuers or captors to discover what their motives and attitude to the dreamer might be.

## CLIMBING/ASCENDING

Climbing without reaching a goal indicates that we may be striving for something we suspect is unobtainable. These can be lofty ideals or unrealistic ambitions adopted in order to compensate for a childhood fear. Alternatively, we may be seeking to rise above the mass of humanity for either altruistic or selfish ends. It would be worthwhile trying to re-enter the dream by active imagination, preferably upon waking, to understand the motive and to see what we are struggling towards or away from.

Climbing a ladder frequently represents professional or social ambitions, whereas a mountain represents life in general. Stairs had only a sexual connotation for Freud, but if the style, steepness and state of the stairs seems significant it can be seen as symbolic of the path ahead. Reaching the top suggests intellectual achievement, while descending the stairs indicates being ready to confront one's deepest fears.

Riding upwards in an elevator is suggestive of a rather functional attitude towards the

sexual act. In any other environment, rising indicates increasing self-awareness. If the feeling is so real that it could almost be physical, then it is almost certainly an out-of-body-experience.

## FLYING

Flight is a common characteristic of lucid dreams in which we have a sudden realization that we are dreaming and that we are able to fly because it is 'only a dream'. These dreams are often exhilarating and accompanied by a sense of infinite possibilities and freedom which has led the mystically inclined to associate them with unconscious astral projection (see pages 28–29).

However, Freud theorized that flying dreams were the dreamer's recollections of being playfully tossed in the air during childhood or of swinging games, both of which awaken sexual feelings we subconsciously wish to recall.

If a difficult decision had been reached prior to falling asleep the flight symbol can be taken as an indication that the subconscious is saying that it is the right decision at the moment. If the dream follows a happy event or an achievement, it reflects a sense of confidence and also a deep sense of relief.

To dream of being a passenger in an aircraft suggests that you are only prepared to explore new opportunities if you do not have to relinquish control or commit yourself too heavily. This dream has the opposite meaning if you are the pilot: that you feel in control of your life and are ready to 'spread your wings'.

## DESCENDING OR BURROWING

An explorative descent into a cave or a hole in the ground suggests a desire to retrieve a repressed memory. The anxiety that we might feel in descending into the darkness does not necessarily indicate that the memory itself is one to be feared, but rather that retrieving it might force us to acknowledge our vulnerability and reassess our self-image.

If the descent is accompanied by a suffocating sense of dread, the dream is likely to indicate a fear of losing oneself in a situation from which there is no obvious way out. If this is the case it could be resolved by re-entering the dream, preferably immediately upon waking, and imagining a positive outcome.

## WAITING

Dreams of waiting for buses, trains and planes are commonplace among regular commuters and travellers. However, it is important to be able to differentiate between dreams of daily routine and those in which the unconscious is using the routine imagery of commuting to convey significant messages.

Dreaming of hurrying to catch a connection and missing it indicates that you may be too ambitious and afraid of failure. If you spend much of your dream time waiting, this indicates that you are not making the most of the opportunities that are presenting themselves, and that you are running the risk of disappointment if the further opportunities for which you are waiting turn out not to be what you hoped for.

It might be worth trying to re-enter the dream using active imagination and catch the connection to see what you missed. It may be that the people on the bus, train or plane are not looking forward to arriving at their destination and that you are better off not trying to catch them up.

## LEARNING

If the dream involves you sitting an exam it suggests an anxiety about being tested or interrogated about your beliefs. Usually, however, the dream is simply reflecting the fear of returning to your schooldays with all the pressures to perform to a required standard. If the scenery has a sense of otherworldliness and the experience you have is unexpectedly pleasant with a sense that something wonderful has been imparted, mystics would suggest that the dreamer has in fact visited a heavenly academy while asleep.

## PACKING

Packing clothes and personal possessions into a trunk or suitcase in a deliberate unhurried way indicates that you are organized, practical and preparing for changes in your life. If the case is bursting, you may be trying to pack too much into your life, or unable to decide what is of real value. If the scene develops into a travel dream the inference is that the situation has become stale and that personal growth will only come if you accept the need for change.

## SWIMMING

The factors of note here are whether you were swimming against the current, whether you were anxious about what might be lurking under the surface and whether you felt adrift or supported by the water. Being surrounded or immersed in refreshing, calm water can be seen as feeling loved and secure. Drifting in water may indicate the need to be fluid in a situation.

Water is an ancient universal symbol of fertility, purity and potential, traditionally signifying the cleansing of past failings prior to being reborn.

## RIDING

Riding is symbolic of sexual intercourse and also of mastery over whatever or whoever is being ridden. If the rider is thrown it indicates a fear of losing control, particularly in a relationship, whereas if the rider is being ridden they have an innate fear of being controlled.

## SAILING

The sailing analogy is traditionally interpreted in conjunction with well-worn phrases such as 'plain sailing', 'sailing too close to the wind' and 'trimming one's sails' where the state of the water is taken to reflect optimism (calm seas) or caution (stormy waters). However, greater insight into one's state of mind may be gained from looking at the type of boat, its condition, whether there was any crew aboard and, if so, noting the captain's character (see 'Dream Quest' visualisation exercise, page 25–27).

## EATING

The way the dreamer is eating should be seen as being equally important to what is being eaten. Eating too much and in a hurry suggests a hunger for affection and a sense of insecurity. If you are on a diet, a dream 'binge' can be dismissed as wish-fulfilment. Eating meagrely and self-consciously indicates a lack of self-worth. Tearing savagely at the food symbolizes the desire to destroy something which is causing stress in waking life. A less frantic approach could mean the desire to ingest the strength of whatever is being eaten.

It is worthwhile examining the characteristics of the other participants, if there are any, as

this hints at the need to integrate their qualities into the personality.

## UNDRESSING

Undressing in public indicates that the dreamer feels restricted and subconsciously harbours a desire to throw off inhibitions and discard conventions and conditioning, in search of a new identity. If the attendant emotion was one of unease, it could indicate a fear of being ridiculed or exposed for imagined failings. The reaction of any spectators could be revealing, but before any significance is attached to the episode the possibility of a 'dream pun' should be considered. Could it be hinting that you should get down to the 'bare essentials' of a problem or reveal the 'naked truth' in order to get something off your mind?

## COMMITTING A CRIME

To dream of committing a crime is quite common and can cause considerable anxiety. The worry is that such a dream might indicate that we will inadvertently commit a crime in the future, or that it is indicating repressed impulses. Such a dream can also relate to a fear of being falsely accused of something or of being persecuted for an inadvertent error. However, the most likely meaning is that the dream represents a comparatively insignificant action in the distant past which we have regretted for so long that it has been magnified

by the subconscious to the point where it now demands to be dealt with.

## WALKING

Walking dreams are generally symbolic of life's journey and the progress made. The most significant factor about them is the character of the landscape. If the scene is of pleasant countryside, this suggests peace of mind and acceptance that one is making the right decisions. If, however, it is an arduous trek through impenetrable jungle or through a busy city the dream might be indicating that your ambitions are unclear, or that you are trying to force your will against the natural flow of events.

Other factors to consider are whether you are continually looking back or striding forward with confidence. Moreover, is there a goal in sight? If so, what is it and how far away does it appear to be? Is the territory ahead difficult, treacherous and intimidating or clear and inviting?

## DECORATING

The process of decorating and renovating a building indicates that it might be time for us to get our own house in order, to clean out old attitudes and conditioning. The colour(s) of the paint and wallpaper could be significant, as could the particular rooms being renewed. If the parts of the house being

dreamt about are utility areas on the ground floor, such as the boiler room, kitchen or bathroom, these might be indicative of the need for us to look more closely into the state of our health. Examination of the upper rooms might yield insights into our mental and spiritual state. The type of house and any furniture within view would give further clues as to our self-image and state of mind (see 'Dream House of the Psyche' exercise on pages 24–25).

## GAMES

Freud thought that most games had sexual connotations, although current thinking favours the idea that it is the relationship between the players that is being highlighted in such dreams. It would be worthwhile examining the attitude of those involved in the game as well as the outcome, if there is one. More revealing detail could be gleaned from an authority figure in the guise of an official or an audience and the effect these have on the players. Spectators on the sidelines and the part they are thought to play in the relationship could also be of great significance.

Competitive games are self-explanatory. Athletic sports might indicate hurdles to overcome, a reluctance to submit to the 'team spirit' at work or in the family, or an urge to cast off a burden as symbolized by throwing a discus, javelin or lifting weights.

## DIGGING

Digging in a garden for the purpose of planting or uprooting a plant usually indicates a need for reorganization and renewal. However, the plant in question may be significant, so this should be looked at. The analogy is clear if we are digging in search of something, but again, the object of the search could be revealing. If the search is frustrated or interrupted, something that we feel is important or of value is not being resolved.

## RESCUING

To dream of rescuing someone usually indicates a secret desire to have that person recognize the heroic qualities which we believe ourselves to possess. However, such a dream can also suggest that behind the selfless heroism there is a wish to have power over the person we rescued, by having them feel indebted to us. This dream might represent an unconscious desire to make amends for putting others in difficulties.

## SEARCHING

Contrary to popular belief, a dream in which you are searching for something does not always indicate that you want to find what you are looking for! The dream ego may know what it is searching for and where to find it, but it may fear the consequences of finding it and so it may make a pretence of searching.

## GAMBLING

Dreams of gambling are traditionally seen as a warning not to take risks. However, if the theme is a card game, it is more likely to indicate that we are indecisive about confiding in someone, wary of 'laying all our cards on the table'. The Puritans viewed card games as the epitome of idleness, while medieval clerics viewed them as a means of education when backed by suitable texts. It may be enlightening to consider which of these types of gambler you consider yourself to be!

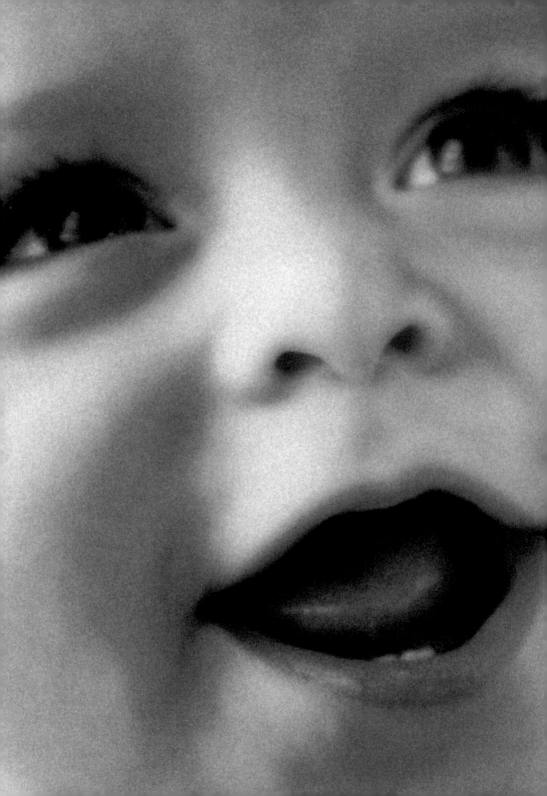

# Body and Soul

DREAMS FEATURING parts of the body as prominent elements should be examined on three levels for possible meanings: the physical, the symbolic, and as compensation for disabilities or perceived failings. In the first category are dreams which may have been triggered by an ailment which has not yet manifested itself.

The physical appearance of the people we meet in our dreams reflects and often exaggerates specific aspects of their personality and our perception of them. Rarely do we 'see' people in their complex entirety as whole beings in dreams. The dream ego, as it is called, can be likened to a two-dimensional cartoon character, often with a serious message.

When attempting to analyse dreams in which facial features have predominated, it is worth remembering that the unconscious often disguises its messages with visual puns. If, for example, you dream that you are on the guillotine or have your head stuck between railings, your unconscious may be trying to tell you your friends believe that you 'are always sticking your neck out'.

The upper part of the body is considered to represent the mental and spiritual aspects of people, while the lower portion represents their instincts and sexual impulses. Dreams which focus on the lower part of the body are drawing our attention to the idea that we may have to reconcile our sensual or anti-social impulses with our higher ideals in order to achieve balance.

## SHOULDERS

Dreams of shouldering a heavy burden invariably imply a weight of responsibility or duties in waking life. How this situation is managed in the dream is indicative of how we are coping in real life. By re-entering the dream we might find someone to share the burden, or we might even make an inventory of what we are carrying and discover that some of it is no longer of value and can be left behind.

## STOMACH

The solar plexus is the centre of the emotions and any problem focusing on this area relates to repressed emotions which need to be released.

## PUTTING ON WEIGHT

If the dream is not related to obvious concerns about a diet, or about fitness and health in general, dreams of putting on excessive weight may represent the dreamer's unconscious apprehension of pregnancy.

## ANUS

Emptying the bowels is a symbol of the ego originating from early childhood when defecating was a way of gaining a reaction from a parent or adult. It can indicate that the ego has been suppressed and needs to re-assert itself, that we feel the need to purge ourselves of inhibitions, or it can indicate an anti-social attitude, wilfulness and defiance of conformity.

## BLOOD

Blood is a universal symbol of the physical and spiritual life-force. For the Orthodox Christian it can refer to the blood of Christ and the act of taking communion with the divine aspect of the self. If in the dream there is a sense of repulsion at bathing, being baptized or covered in blood, however, the suggestion is a fear of taking responsibility and entering into adulthood.

For a man to dream that he is bleeding from a wound the suggestion is fear of emasculation, humiliation and loss of virility. The same dream for a woman suggests the fear of losing her virginity or the memory of that event. Wounds can also represent emotional trauma, especially fear of being emotionally 'drained' by a lover, or of suffering self-inflicted wounds through rash actions.

If the wounds leave a scar, the implication is that the emotional effects have not yet been dealt with. If they are seen to heal, this is reassurance that the dreamer has the capacity for self-healing.

## EYE

The eye is symbolic of higher consciousness and relates to the belief that we all have an invisible 'third eye' in the centre of our foreheads between the eyebrows which is the gateway to a psychic sixth sense.

Loss of sight indicates the loss of psychic and spiritual perception, or a missed opportunity to gain greater perception due to a fear of, or an unwillingness to relinquish, materialistic values. The regaining of sight has the opposite meaning, but can also indicate that a decision recently made offers considerable potential.

On a mundane level, seeing your own eyes closed in a dream implies that you do not want to face the truth in a situation or that you are blind to the possibilities before you.

## NOSE

Symbolically the nose relates to intuition, hence the phrases 'to sniff something out' and 'I can smell that something isn't right'; Freudians, though, would limit the nose to a phallic symbol. When analyzing dreams which feature noses in an unusually prominent way, it is worth remembering the obvious visual connotations. These might be looking down the nose at everyone else (being condescending), holding one's nose in the air (haughtiness) or poking the nose into other people's business (intrusiveness).

## HAIR

Freudians believe that head or body hair is a displacement symbol for pubic hair and therefore a symbol of sexual potency. Dreams in which the hair falls out or the dreamer discovers that he is bald would indicate a fear of impotency or the loss of physical strength.

## LIMBS

Limbs can have a phallic connotation. The loss of a limb may represent loss of virility for a male or loss of virginity for a female. Being dismembered symbolizes the fear that one's life is coming apart, although it may simply indicate the necessity for reassessment.

Outstretched arms imply a need for help, support or acceptance. In a dream of this kind it would be necessary to consider whose arms are reaching out to whom and for what purpose.

Legs are more likely to appear as pictorial puns on well-known phrases. For example, if the dreamer has been drinking heavily they may dream that they are literally 'legless'.

Similarly, dreaming that your feet are frozen is likely to play on the phrase 'having cold feet', implying second thoughts concerning an agreement.

## HANDS

The hands symbolize creative potential in the sense of crafting physical objects and, as hands can be read as another phallic symbol, creating life. When the dreamer finds a different object in each hand, or is weighing the contents of one hand against the other, it signifies that a difficult decision has to be made – the contents of the left hand will often represent what is best for the mind or heart and those in the right hand what is best for physical security, comfort or material gain. Dirty hands imply a guilty conscience, and washing them suggests we desire to be rid of guilt or an association which makes us feel uncomfortable.

## PENIS

The penis is symbolic of the life-force. However, the presence of phallic imagery as a dominant and recurring theme in a series of dreams implies that we are either undervaluing our sexuality or maybe even ignoring its existence altogether.

Although it is the sexual function which is invariably being implied by the appearance of the penis, urinating or the need to urinate in a dream can represent the need to express or bottle up the emotions. Urinating is believed to be an infantile form of sexuality when the means of expressing emotion were limited to bodily functions.

## MOUTH

The mouth is a potent symbol of our demands and our needs, although Freudians would limit these to sexual desires, seeing the mouth itself as a symbol of the female genitalia and the tongue as a symbol of the penis.

If the focus of the dream is on eating, attention should be paid to the significance of what is being eaten and the way it is being consumed (see Eating, page 36).

## SKIN

A dream focusing on the skin, such as being naked or having tattoos, serves the same purpose as dreams in which the emphasis is on clothes. Both skin and clothes are symbolic of the persona; how we perceive ourselves and how we believe others see us. Exposing the skin is generally indicative of showing emotions. Having tender skin marked or scarred symbolizes vulnerability. A dream including tough skin would suggest strong emotional defences.

## HEAD

The head is often symbolic of the dreamer's intellect and intentions. A disproportionately large head, for example, indicates an inflated ego. Seeing one's own head in a dream may be an unconscious prompt to 'get ahead' or 'use your head' in resolving a particular situation, although it can also be symbolic of the head of a business or organization with which the dreamer is involved.

## FACE

We may be adept at hiding our emotions in waking life, but in our dreams the faces we see, though rarely our own, frequently reflect our true feelings and our perception of the way that others see us. If we are confronted by an accusing look in the dream world, we can be sure that we are harbouring some disapproval of something we said or did that day. Likewise, if we see a shadowy character whose face is half-hidden in the gloom, or if we meet a shabby individual with a grubby face in our dreams, we can be sure that he or she is a reflection of our shame. Conversely, if our dreams are filled with happy, smiling faces, we can assume that we are inwardly content and have reason to be optimistic.

## TEETH

A full set of healthy teeth is a symbol of our ability to eat whatever we choose and thus sustain ourselves. Losing teeth in a dream usually represents a fear of becoming helpless. Such imagery can be particularly distressing because it implies there might be something rotten or diseased in a sensitive area of our lives or body (see Mouth). However, if this image is accompanied by a feeling of relief, the inference to be drawn from the dream is that the problem festering away in the psyche has finally been removed. Teeth falling out easily in the dream is a flashback to childhood when the loss of teeth was a sign of impending maturity and the end of a comparatively carefree existence. Perhaps the dreamer has a secret wish to return to those carefree days?

The loss of teeth accompanied by embarrassment and anxiety indicates that we subconsciously fear what old age might bring – helplessness, impoverishment, undesirability, ill-health and dependency. However, as our teeth help shape our features, yet another interpretation can be read into this image – fear of 'losing face'.

Freudians would also see a sexual connotation, with the teeth representative of aggressive sexuality, especially in dreams where the act of biting is a feature. Conversely, a dream in which a woman swallows a tooth would be seen by Freudians as being symbolic of her desire for or fear of pregnancy.

## CLOTHES

Even if we are not consciously aware of the fact, it is nevertheless true that we choose our clothes as outward expressions of our attitudes, circumstances and emotions. It is only when we are forced into a uniform that our individuality and uniqueness is supplanted by what that uniform represents to others. Our choice of clothes can reflect an attempt to compensate for a lack of self-confidence and sense of identity, such as when children and adolescents adopt the dress style of their peers and idols.

It is important to note how people in our dreams are dressed and whether they might be attempting to disguise their true

nature or feelings by what appears to be an inappropriate choice of clothes for them or the situation in which you see them. Is it possible that they are wearing heavy coats as a thick skin against the unpredictable elements of life, or large hats and glasses to obscure their faces?

Formal dress suggests that there are inhibitions, constraints and rigid attitudes. Period costume implies a tendency to dwell on the past or a dislike of their present circumstances.

New clothes represent self-confidence, whereas old, dirty or dishevelled clothes represent a negative self-image and deep sense of insecurity.

Seeing someone you know in the uniform of an authority figure indicates that you consider them to be officious and overbearing. If a partner occasionally appears dressed as a child in your dreams, this suggests that you find them immature at times.

One of the most common dreams in which clothes betray the character is where the dreamer finds himself dressed in entirely the wrong outfit for a particular occasion. This dream scenario represents the fear of making a social blunder or committing an indiscretion.

If a sense of fulfilment and pleasure accompanies your choice of clothes in a dream, this may indicate that the time has come for you to reconsider your self-image, to acknowledge your

qualities and express these in your outward appearance.

## UNDERWEAR

Dreaming of finding oneself in a public place dressed only in underwear is actually one of the commonest anxiety dreams and of no great significance. On the other hand, however, to dream of wearing comic or novelty underwear in the presence of a lover indicates that the dreamer is either immature, embarrassed by sex or does not take the relationship seriously.

Exotic lingerie suggests hidden passion. Dull or discoloured lingerie might suggest low self-esteem, feelings of unworthiness or disappointment with the romantic aspect of life.

## SHOES

Shoes are symbols of progress and travel. Buying new shoes can indicate a desire for change and adventure. Indecision about which pair to purchase, or having too many to choose from, suggests a lack of direction in waking life.

Not being able to find a pair of shoes indicates a fear of not being ready when an opportunity arises. The type and condition of the shoes can say much about your present progress. Heavy, ungainly footwear could indicate that you sense you are 'dragging your feet' or tripping yourself up to avoid having to do something or go somewhere. Shiny new

shoes are a symbol of high self-esteem. Worn shoes represent anxiety about money and low self-esteem. Tying one's shoelaces securely reflects new-found confidence. Seeing tangled or untied shoelaces in a dream could reflect a number of loose ends which need to be secured or they might trip you up.

## MASKS

Masks are worn in dreams for the same reason they are worn in the waking world – to disguise the identity and nature of the person wearing it. If you were wearing the mask, consider why you felt the need to do so. What were you trying to hide from the world? If the mask was being worn by someone you know, could it be that your image of them is not a true likeness? Are you trying to project qualities onto them which you would like them to possess, but which you subconsciously suspect they do not have?

## MAKE-UP

Applying cosmetics (other than lipstick, which has erotic connotations) for either aesthetic or theatrical purposes indicates the desire to remodel one's image. The motivation for this could be deceit and disguise if the make-up is accompanied by a change of costume and other items which render the dreamer unrecognizable.

## HATS

Although relatively few people wear hats these days, other than as part of a uniform, they can feature in our dreams as symbols of status because of associations with their use in the past.

Wearing or being offered a crown symbolizes achievement, ambition and high self-esteem. Top hats are indicative of social status and the need to make an impression. Cloth caps imply a level-headed working-class attitude and lack of pretence. Having your hat stolen or damaged can mean that you fear that someone might threaten your position either at work or socially. In that case, you should re-enter the dream upon waking and allow your imagination to track down and uncover who it is and why they might want to do this.

## BIRTH

Although it is extremely rare to dream of being born, it is fairly common to have dreams which are symbolic of the processes of birth and the trauma which accompanied our birth or the birth of our own children.

There is now considerable evidence that we retain vivid memories of our own birth deep within the unconscious and that these can resurface in our dreams, if and when we experience a trauma of equal intensity. Birth images may be reversed, with the dreamer crawling into or out of small tunnels or holes in a state of apprehension, or diving into or emerging from the sea. These dreams are more likely to reflect anxiety concerning the present situation than the birth that they are recalling.

Dreaming of an embryo in the womb symbolizes a future pregnant with possibilities, but that the dreamer is reluctant to 'grow up' and leave the security which the present situation appears to offer. If, however, in your dream you are the witness to a birth, it indicates a desire to have the chance to live life over again for the purpose of avoiding past mistakes.

For a woman, dreams of giving birth generally signify fulfilment, perhaps the fruition of an idea which had been in gestation for some time, or even the need for a complete change in our lives (see The Dream Journey, page 16).

## BABIES

For anyone other than an expectant or anxious parent of young children, babies are symbolic of a cherished idea or new venture which the dreamer is considering.

A persistently crying child would indicate that the dreamer finds the idea unsettling and is concerned about the increased demands it might make on their time and finances.

Being present at a premature birth or being ill-prepared for a birth also suggests anxiety about the project. More preparation and thought might allay the fears associated with these dreams and thus bring an end to them.

## CHILDREN

Just as we place our hopes in our children in waking life so do we symbolically in the children who feature in our dreams. Dream children can personify our own 'inner child', the hopes and beliefs we cherished as children and still secretly nurture deep within our psyche. They can also represent the work we do, the ideas we have and anything else that expresses who we are and what we wish to send out into the world.

## ILLNESS

There is an old theory, now supported by recent scientific research, which holds that all physical illness is caused by inner mental conflict and repressed emotions. It is an extension of the theory of psychosomatic sickness which says that some illnesses appear to originate in the mind and may even manifest themselves to gain the sufferer attention or sympathy in extreme cases. Now it is suggested that the unconscious intentionally brings illness into being in order to call our attention to a particular problem

and that by paying attention to the message in our dreams we may relieve ourselves of what is essentially 'dis-ease'.

Dreams that are concerned with physical illness can be seen as symbolizing emotional turmoil or mental conflict which might manifest in physical illness if it is not positively resolved. Dreams involving painful stomach cramps and ulcers, for example, suggest that the dreamer's frustration has turned inwards and is eating away at their insides.

An examination of the specific imagery of the dream should give a clue as to the underlying cause of the problem and probably will hint at a possible 'cure'.

## HUNGER AND THIRST

Freudians believe that the appetites are substitutes for sexual desire and that sharing a meal with someone in a dream symbolizes the dreamer's desire to have sex with that person. They even interpret a visit to a restaurant as a secret wish to visit a brothel!

It is more likely, however, that appetites are symbols of a hunger or thirst for something that the dreamer does not possess at present, such as a house similar to the one in which the meal takes place, the money necessary to pay for similar luxuries, the ability to be at ease socially without being self-conscious, or even the undivided attention of the person they are dining with.

## PREGNANCY

If a dream of becoming pregnant is accompanied by a pleasing feeling of anticipation, it signifies hope for the future and a sense of infinite possibilities. However, if the dream is disturbing, the indication is fear of responsibility, missed opportunities and of having to face the consequences of past actions.

## OPERATIONS

Surgery indicates unwillingness to submit to the will of another or to have one's way of life interfered with or beliefs challenged.

## CASTRATION

A common anxiety dream among men who fear the responsibilities of adulthood, but are at the same time anxious about proving their manhood to their peers and their partners. Dreaming of castration can also signify anxieties related to many aspects of male sexuality, including fear of latent homosexuality and the impotence of old age. On a different level, it might suggest that there is a conflict between the masculine and feminine aspects of the personality, possibly because the man is attempting to deny his feminine side with the result that this asserts itself in aggressive imagery during his sleep.

## DEATH

Dreaming of the death of a loved one can serve as a release of the repressed hostility which occurs in even the most affectionate relationships. This mechanism originates from childhood when intense emotions could not be fully expressed and were not tempered with guilt or remorse.

Dreaming of the death of a parent expresses the conflicting feelings common to all parent-child relationships, intensified by the mother/daughter rivalry for the father's affection and the father/son rivalry for attention from the mother.

Although the image of death can represent a wish on behalf of the dreamer to be rid of someone, it can also represent the dreamer's destructive tendencies – for example, his or her anger and frustration at life in general – and have nothing to do with the identity of the deceased.

Some dreams of death do not symbolize the negative feelings of the dreamer for that person in waking life. The dreamer could be considered to be anticipating the absence of the loved one in order to examine the depth of their own feelings towards them.

If you dream of your own death a likely explanation is that you feel that the demands of life are draining you of your vitality or that you consider yourself to be unappreciated by others and may as well put yourself into a state where nothing more is demanded

or expected of you. Death implies bereavement and a reassessment of life, suggesting a secret wish to have others feel guilty for not appreciating our qualities. If the atmosphere in the dream is positive, it may be that the dreamer's old attitudes are being peacefully put to rest in anticipation of a rebirth. More clues can be obtained from looking at the attitude of the mourners, if there are any, and the state of the body. If rigor mortis has set in the implication is a rigid attitude and crippling apprehension about what life might demand.

To face the figure of Death itself, as the Grim Reaper or another archetype, is to face the fact of one's own mortality.

## SPIRITUAL IMAGERY

The difficulty in interpreting the significance of religious images in dreams is that the unconscious may be drawing our attention to their esoteric (hidden or inner) rather than their exoteric (external or traditional) meaning. An understanding of both and their personal significance for the dreamer is therefore necessary to reveal the full extent of what the unconscious is trying to tell us. Dreams that are strong in religious symbolism are more common to those who have denied their own spiritual nature in the belief that they are only rejecting religious dogma and conformism. As a result their inner being is trying to reassert itself by projecting the strongest images in its memory.

Those who shun the material world and all its attractions will find themselves tormented in their dreams by gross caricatures of the instincts and passions they are attempting to suppress. It is worth bearing in mind that the unconscious can also draw on religious imagery as a metaphor for secular concepts – the image of a biblical prophet, for example, to contrast past and present or use of an idol or divine figure to represent someone the dreamer subconsciously admires!

## ANGELS

Some people believe that the appearance of an angel in a dream signifies contact with a benign discarnate entity or the dreamer's Higher Self and that any message that is conveyed should be taken seriously. Others view angelic images as symbolizing an idyllic view of women or the desire to spread one's own wings and make dramatic changes in life.

## SPIRITUAL ICONS

A dream visitation from a great spiritual and religious leader may have the same meaning as that of an angelic being. However, such a dream will have a distinct resonance and significance for the individual dreamer. The appearance of Moses, for example, may be prompting the

dreamer to consider the implications of breaking one of the basic commandments. Buddha has become a symbol of inner strength, and Jesus a sacrificial figure. But these are only the most immediate interpretations. It would be necessary for the dreamer to examine his or her present situation in detail to discover the relevance of the vision.

## RELIGIOUS BUILDINGS

Many places of worship, including some of the most impressive cathedrals in Europe, were designed upon ancient esoteric principles which would have been understood by initiates but which have now been largely forgotten even by orthodox priests and their most devout congregations. Many of the major world religions incorporated their secret teachings into the design of their churches and temples to preserve them in times of persecution and to give their initiates material for contemplation. Synagogues, for example, are still built to designs which represent the four worlds which the Jewish mystics of ancient times believed symbolized the structure of existence, although few orthodox Jews are aware of these symbols and their significance today. According to Carl Jung (see pages 14–16), we can all tap into the Collective Unconscious where such secrets are to be found. The

most propitious time to do this is when we are dreaming.

If religious images are a frequent feature of your dreams, it might be worthwhile studying the esoteric teachings of your tradition or belief to search for those hidden meanings. Revelations are not exclusively for the religious!

# Colours

WE ALL DREAM in colour. The colours we dream in can be as significant as the objects, events and people that we dream about.

As long ago as 1940 Dr Max Luscher devised a colour test which proved that we decorate our homes and choose the colour of our clothes – and even our cars – to correspond with our psychological make-up. More recent research has shown that colours can affect our moods and even our health. Blue, for example, has a calming effect, whereas red is stimulating both physiologically and psychologically. However, in our dreams it is not only our preferences and our moods that are encoded in colour, but also the quality of energy which those people or objects possess, as perceived by our own unconscious. Bright, primary colours reflect vitality and a positive outlook, whereas pastoral shades suggest serenity and dull colours indicate depression.

## GOLD

Gold has many associations with wealth, refinement and divinity. In the ancient world it was considered the purest and most precious of minerals because of its association with the sun, its radiant beauty and for the fact that it could not be corrupted by rust. Gold symbolized the vibrant male sun god and thus strength. Through the ages it embodied all the attributes of heavenly glory and earthly power. It was the chosen metal in the making of sacred objects and its creation from base material was the ultimate goal of the alchemists.

To dream of a person arraigned in gold is to be thinking of them in the highest terms. Such a dream signifies secret respect and admiration for that person rather than affection. To dream of mining for gold indicates that something of great significance has been buried in the unconscious. The discovery of more gold than we can carry in a dream suggests that we are trying to do more than is practical in the mistaken belief that activity equals achievement.

## SILVER

In the ancient world, silver was regarded as the second most precious metal. It was the complement of gold, representing the cool mysterious feminine goddess personified as the moon. To dream of silver is considered to indicate purity, chastity and the talent to charm (hence the popular term 'to be silver-tongued').

## WHITE

Pure white light is said to be a true reflection of divine primordial energy. White is traditionally associated with pure energy and is used in Yoga and other Indian esoteric philosophies to represent the highest (crown) chakra, or subtle energy centre, in the etheric body. To dream of white is to dream of the highest potential of whatever the dreamer is imagining. In psychological terms white symbolizes the importance of the intellect.

## VIOLET

Violet is a transitional colour in practical, psychological and spiritual terms, being a blend of red (symbolizing physical energy, fire and action) with blue (symbolizing the sea or sky, the celestial and the intellect). In ancient Rome violets were worn on the heads of banqueting guests in order to to cool and calm them. This custom led to the colour becoming associated with the desirable qualities of moderation and a balance of passion with aspiration.

## PURPLE

The ancient Romans reserved this rarest of dyes for their emperors, and also for persons of rank, such as magistrates, military leaders and priests.

In dreams the subconscious might therefore draw on the colour's associations with dignity, authority and force. If the image in the dream comes from a deeper level it might be drawing upon the colour's spiritual significance. In spiritual and psychic terms purple is a primary healing colour and the colour most often associated with the third eye, or gateway to the etheric realms, which is located between the eyebrows. A dream involving purple might signify that the psychic senses are awakening, so you can expect significant coincidences, fortuitous meetings and other enlightening experiences in the months ahead.

## BLUE

Blue is the third primary colour and the first of the spiritual colours. There is a strong folk tradition in Europe which associates the colour blue with fidelity. This is echoed by the Chinese belief that the appearance of the colour in a dream is a portent of a happy and enduring marriage. To dream of a prominent vivid blue object, cloudless sky or serene seascape can be interpreted as a message from the unconscious that the veil to the subconscious can now be lifted at will.

From a psychological perspective light blue is most commonly associated with the sky and the sea, both of which

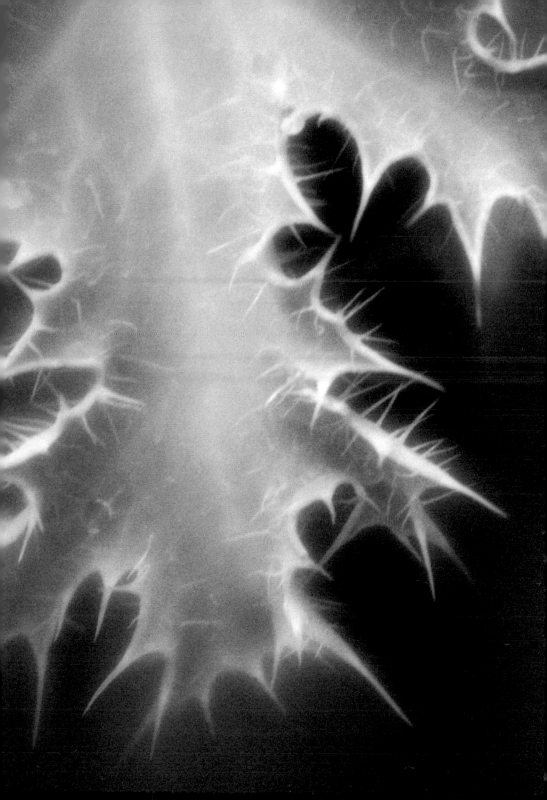

are elements concerned with mutable emotions. The association of the colour blue with the sky is also suggestive of elevated, spiritual thoughts and intuition, implying that the unconscious is likely to be urging the dreamer to trust his or her intuition in a matter where the emotions are concerned. A dream featuring the colour of calm seas and fair skies appears to promise a positive outcome.

Despite its popular association with melancholy, deep blue is a calming and healing colour associated with the throat chakra in eastern philosophies. Its presence in a dream implies the need for self-expression for the purpose of healing oneself and others who might be touched by the beauty of whatever is created. Perhaps the dreamer has crippling doubts about his or her ability or self-worth and could be healed through some form of creative expression.

## GREEN

Green has a number of negative associations such as envy, inexperience and jealousy, but it is also the universal symbol of spring, freshness and vitality. In occult philosophy it is seen as the colour of harmony, balance and regeneration as embodied in nature. It corresponds to the quality of energy at the heart chakra and is the frequency between the physical and the spiritual realms. This is one reason why we seek to find harmony, balance and peace in a garden and in the countryside.

In practical terms it is the colour which we have come to associate with safety and permission to proceed, as in the green of traffic lights and the international green cross adopted by the pharmaceutical industry. Green has dual meanings in dreams – lushness and coolness – and requires careful interpretation. A dream featuring a significant green element might be urging you to get on with a pet project or seek fresh opportunities further afield. Or, it might be cautioning against the belief that the grass is always greener on the other side of the fence!

## YELLOW

Yellow is the second of the primary colours. In ancient times it was associated with the life-giving force and healing rays of the sun. It corresponds to the third chakra at the level of the solar plexus which is associated with the emotions.

In dreamlore yellow is more likely to reflect nervous energy, repressed emotions, intellectual achievement and ambition. If your dream features someone in yellow, this person could represent someone who excites strong emotions within you, perhaps because you strongly disagree with their opinions or consider them to be overly critical and lacking in spontaneity.

## ORANGE

Orange comes between the red of the physical dimension and the yellow of the mental aspects of our being and is the colour of positive emotions. Orange is associated with fire and the setting sun, both suggesting controlled passion. Orange blossoms were once bound in bridal bouquets as tokens of fertility, and the Chinese traditionally eat oranges at New Year as symbols of good fortune.

## RED

Red is the lowest vibration of the colour spectrum and the first of the three primary colours. It corresponds to the lower chakra at the base of the spine and is the colour of physical energy, of action and the passions. In the physical world it is the colour we associate with blood, fire, heat and danger and yet the more pastel shades are considered symbolic of the finer aspects of physical energy (as in those energies needed in sport) while the darker reds symbolize the more intense emotions such as passion and anger.

It is no arbitrary association or coincidence that has led to the heart, as the seat of the passions, being popularly but erroneously depicted as red.

## BROWN

Brown is associated with the earth and with many hibernating animals. It may appear in dreams to symbolize a period of inactivity and rest prior to sowing the seeds of the next harvest in life.

If we dream of someone in mousy brown clothes this could indicate that we consider them to be shy, modest and unassuming, although appearances can be deceptive! The usual meaning is impoverishment, because brown is the colour of barren soil and the habits of poor Christian monks.

## GREY

Almost colourless, grey reminds us of ashes and lifelessness. It should not be forgotten, however, that out of ashes can come new life and regeneration. A dream focusing on a grey object, landscape or item of clothing might appear to suggest that all is drab and lacking in vitality, but it could equally be an encouragement to us to consider how we can bring colour and energy back into our life.

## BLACK

Light is reduced by degrees until the polar opposite of white is reached – black, in essence the absence of light, associated with negativity, evil and death.

Black is associated with death in Western society because it signifies the belief that the divine light of the life force has departed. (In many cultures of the East, however, white is associated with death, it being symbolic of the soul's return to the divine light.) Crows, ravens, cats and even black stallions are traditionally considered to be creatures of ill omen.

For orthodox Christians blackbirds are the symbol of temptation. Christian and Muslim clerics wear black to symbolize that they have renounced the attractions of the world. In esoteric and occult circles black is held to be the colour of the physical world, being the densest colour and our world being the densest plane of energy.

Black has a secondary symbolic significance and that is secrecy. The unconscious might shield a person in the dream in deep shadow or cover an object with a black cloth to indicate that the dreamer is hiding a secret, or that the other person or object is concealing a secret.

## BLACK/WHITE

Because most of our dreams are in colour, it can be assumed that black and white will be used to highlight duality and contrast. Figures dressed predominantly in black or white stand out against a crowd more effectively than any other colour combination and so will be used by the unconscious to draw the dreamer's attention to individuals clothed in either of these colours.

# Numbers

NUMBERS ARE SAID to be the key to cosmic harmony and certain numbers and combinations representative of the divine mysteries. As with colours, each number is believed to correspond to a specific frequency of vibration which is attuned to the rhythmic cycles of the universe. Many ancient alphabets had numerical counterparts and this led to the belief that it was possible to reveal the secret meanings of words through analysis of the corresponding numerical values. Until recently it was even widely believed that the true nature and destiny of an individual could be revealed by decoding the numerical value of his or her name!

However, in dreams the relevant numbers may not appear as recognizable digits for easy analysis but as a group of objects or people whose quantity or grouping has to be recognized as symbolically significant. For example, if the dream features two candlesticks or two pillars the dream relates to the need for balance.

## ODD AND EVEN NUMBERS

Odd numbers are generally representative of the mysterious, intuitive, unknown and unpredictable elements in life, whereas even numbers represent the familiar and practical everyday elements. However, in ancient Greece even numbers were considered to symbolize feminine, passive qualities, and odd numbers the active and masculine qualities.

## DATES

Dreaming of a particular date on a calendar, in a desk diary or newspaper may be a reminder of an important forthcoming event such as a birthday, job interview or anniversary. Such a dream could also be precognitive. It is not uncommon for a housebuyer to dream of the number of the house he or she will later own. In drawing the dreamer's attention to a future day, week or month the dream might be forewarning of changes ahead.

## ZERO

Drawn as a circle, zero represents infinity. In ancient Babylonia, India and Arabia zero was seen as a sacred symbol of the creator, the essence of all things. Its appearance as a significant element in a dream would indicate that all potential is contained within but that the dreamer is waiting for ideal conditions. Its reverse meaning, as a symbol of nothingness, is a warning not to wait too long before taking action.

## ONE

The number one has traditionally symbolized unity and perfection as envisaged in the form of an omnipotent deity. A phallic shape, it can also represent active masculinity and force. One can also suggest the first stage of a journey. More commonly it implies aloofness or isolation. In a competitive context, it promises success and the confidence to put oneself first.

## TWO

Two signifies duality and balance. The symbolism and context will clarify whether the twin aspects, often the dreamer and his or her partner, are in opposition or harmony. If the number is expressed in the form of objects the implication is one of contrast, such as the benefits of reflection as opposed to action. The dreamer should note how the objects appear in relation to each other. If they are seen side by side the configuration suggests equality, whereas if one is behind the other then it implies that one aspect of the dreamer or one person in the relationship is in the shadow of the other.

The number two can also appear as a significant symbol in dreams when the dreamer has a choice to make between two equally appealing alternatives.

## THREE

Traditionally, three symbolizes the harmonious integration of the principal aspects of the individual: mind, body and spirit. In Christianity this is represented by the Trinity. In psychological terms it stands for the id, ego and superego or as our behaviour, feelings and thoughts. In Chinese culture the triad reflects the harmony that exists between earth, man and heaven.

When the number three is expressed as a pyramid it symbolizes the infusion and balance of energy for creativity and spiritual development. Its main function in a dream is to emphasize the importance of trusting intuition and the need to develop inner strength.

The appearance of three people emphasizes the importance that the dreamer places on the family, either as a child with parents or as the parent of a child with a partner with whom he or she feels secure.

## FOUR

Traditionally four corresponds to the four elements (fire, water, earth and air) and also to the cycle of birth and death as reflected in the four seasons. We have each of the elements within us: the gaseousness of our breath, the earthiness of our bones, the liquidity of our blood and the heat in our skin. Four can also symbolize the square that lies at the base of a pyramid,

implying the importance of placing the elements of one's life upon solid foundations.

## FIVE

Five is the symbol of the living spirit, the fully realized human being or the cosmic being in whose image we are made with our five appendages (head, arms and legs) as represented by the occult symbol of the pentagram. Five also symbolizes the five senses. A dream involving this number indicates that we are absorbed in the material world and our own comfort.

## SIX

Six often appears as a phonetic pun for sex in dreams, although it is more commonly representative of the harmonious relationship of male and female attributes within a single individual. In esoteric teachings the male is represented by the upward-pointing triangle and the female by the downward-pointing triangle. The harmonious blending of these six points finds graphic expression in the hexagram or Star of David, a magical symbol now adopted as a national emblem by the state of Israel. The number's association with luck and good fortune stems from its use on six-sided dice and its close association with the I Ching, the ancient Chinese system of divination, of which it forms the basis. Its association with bad luck is pure superstition, probably deriving from the fact

that the 'Book of Revelation' identified Satan's secret number as 666, for no other reason than this number falls repeatedly short of the sacred number seven!

## SEVEN

Seven was a sacred number for the ancients, who acknowledged the existence of seven planets in the solar system and worshipped the seven gods who ruled them.

In Eastern philosophy and esoteric practice there are seven major chakras or subtle energy centres in the human body. A dream focusing on this number could therefore be regarded as hinting at the awakening of hidden wisdom and the balancing of mind, body and spirit.

## EIGHT

Eight is a sacred number, the number of cosmic equilibrium. To dream of an eight-sided object is an augury of good fortune as the octagon is a universal symbol of stability and totality. Eight is also a number associated with inner strength – the lotus, a powerful Buddhist symbol of spiritual unfolding, is usually depicted with eight petals.

## NINE

Nine corresponds to the months of pregnancy in human beings and thereby to regeneration and new possibilities, particularly in the arts and sciences. Each of the nine muses, or planetary goddesses, of ancient Greek

mythology personified one of the attributes needed to succeed in the arts and sciences.

## TEN

As an image the number 10 is suggestive of contrast, with the straight vertical line appearing in opposition to the circle, and is traditionally seen as symbolizing male (1) and female (0). At a deeper level it may be hinting at finality, with the line seen as a barrier impeding the circle's progress and the circle as an image of wholeness and harmony. Perhaps you have completed a phase of your life and can now go no further on your present course?

In the esoteric tradition, ten corresponds to the ten spheres on the Tree of Life, a symbol of the various qualities or attributes of the divine which are reflected in the human psyche and physical body. Dreaming of the number ten is therefore of great spiritual significance for those actively seeking enlightenment. A dream in which this meaningful number features would suggest that the various elements in the dreamer's life are in balance and that a new level of understanding is about to be reached.

## TWELVE

Twelve signifies celestial order and completion of a cycle of activity in terms of time. It may be symbolized by the twelve signs of the zodiac, a calendar representing the twelve months of the year or a clock representing the twelve hours of the day. In some cultures, twelve is the age of maturity and responsibility when a child is accepted by the community as an adult. The sense of self-development and new-found status this represents may express itself in dream symbolism, such as receiving the gift of a watch with the hands fixed at twelve o'clock or, as is often the case, with no hands at all!

## THIRTEEN

Thirteen has become a number of ill omen due to its many negative associations: Judas Iscariot was counted as the thirteenth man present at the Last Supper; the devil has been imagined to be the thirteenth guest of a witches' coven; in pagan mythology the Scandinavian god of light, Balder, was slain at a banquet in Valhalla by an unexpected thirteenth guest, the intruder Loki; in ancient times the addition of an extra, thirteenth, 'month' to complete the early lunar calendars was considered unlucky.

The superstition attached to the number thirteen has been further enforced by other 'meaningful coincidences', such as the fact that the thirteenth Tarot card in the major arcana is Death. However, a more accurate interpretation of this card and of the number 13 appearing in a dream is that both signify change. To dream that you are entering a house or room numbered 13 or ascending to the thirteenth floor, indicates anxiety concerning coming changes, but also an overwhelming curiosity to explore new possibilities.

## FORTY

The phrase 'life begins at forty' has its origins in the belief that a period of forty years is required before a man or woman has sufficient knowledge and experience of the world to renounce its distractions and turn to more spiritual values. Thus Islam, Judaism and Christianity require a 40-day period of purification and preparation, such as fasting, before important religious festivals and rites. The biblical fables also emphasize the importance of the period – there is the legend of the Israelites who wandered in the desert for 40 years to purify themselves for a new beginning in the Promised Land; the Flood which took 40 years to purge the surface of the earth; and Christ spending 40 days fasting in preparation for 40 months preaching.

## ONE HUNDRED

Pictorially 100 suggests an emotional triad, with two women vying for the attention of one male. A more common interpretation is that the number simply stands for an uncountable number, for 'many'.

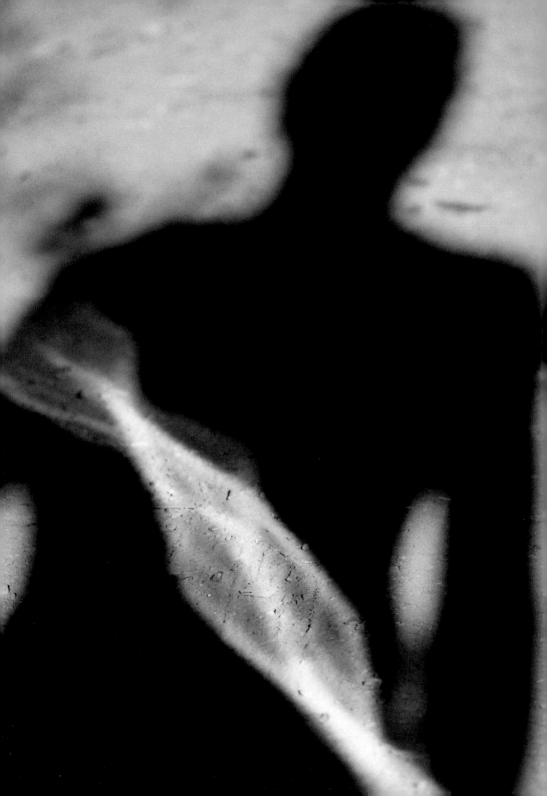

# Personalities and Personas

THE PEOPLE who appear in our dreams may not always be what they seem. Even our partners or close family members may appear as caricatures of the people we think we know so well. Our dreams are largely created from unconscious impressions and so they will frequently reveal how we really see our families and friends. Dreams can, of course, also reveal how we perceive ourselves. To complicate matters and make the interpretation of dreams a real art, we have to appreciate that our unconscious can use people who we know as reflections of ourselves. Even people we do not like may appear not as themselves, but as substitutes or stand-ins for our own foibles and failings which we prefer not to acknowledge.

Other aspects of the personality which may assume a form in the dreamworld are the Shadow Self (the undeveloped or unrecognized aspects), the True Self (the ideal or potential for perfection) and the anima or animus (the qualities of the opposite sex which we all share). Another form which the unconscious uses to embody abstract qualities, attributes or ideals is the archetype – an inherited symbol which is common to us all with only minor cultural variations. The appearance of these figures in our dreams is a sign that one aspect of our personality is in the ascendant. As appealing as it might be to see ourselves in the guise of a king or hero, it is a reminder that we must not allow one aspect to overwhelm and possess us at the expense of the others. All aspects must be integrated into the Greater or True Self if we are to achieve wholeness.

## SHADOW

The Shadow is that part of ourselves which we choose to ignore and which reacts by haunting our dreams. For example, an introvert will often dream of acting in an outrageous fashion, while an extrovert may compensate for time spent impressing others by taking time for him or herself. If we are able to recognize the Shadow when it appears and gradually integrate rather than deny its existence, it will cease to haunt our dreams.

## ANIMA/ANIMUS

The anima manifests when the male has seriously neglected the feminine aspect of his nature (the emotional and intuitive). The animus appears when the female has denied the male characteristics (particularly rationality and discernment).

The form which these abstract qualities assume in our dreams fall into four main types. In the man they are the Father, the Youth, the Hero and the Magician. The four female types are the Mother, the Princess, the Amazon and the Priestess. Each has its negative side and can take on the form of an animal or mythological creature which we perceive as embodying that quality.

## GREAT MOTHER

It is not necessary for a woman to bear children or even desire to be a mother to dream of this archetype. The Great Mother personifies a woman's ultimate integrated Self, the sum of all that she has potential to be. The outwards manifestation of the Great Mother is Nature.

## MOTHER

Dreaming of a mother figure is to face the maternal instinct, namely the desire to nurture and protect the young. It could mean that the unconscious is encouraging us to comfort and nurture the 'inner child'. This is especially the case if we have been too hard on ourselves or have temporarily lost the child-like love of life. However, there are always two sides to each figure and the unconscious may use a mother figure to admonish the dreamer for an act the dreamer knew was wrong but which it was hoped could be got away with.

The unconscious does not respect political correctness and it could even project an image of the mother dutifully carrying out domestic chores to remind a male dreamer of his obligations and responsibilities as a father or son.

On a deeper level the mother is an aspect of female energy, which can assume a form known as the Terrible Mother, often appearing as a wicked queen, witch or a black widow spider. In these forms the mother embodies the negative characteristics of the over-protective and possessive matriarch who smothers her children's potential for growth. A woman who lives her life through her children, sacrificing her happiness in the belief that they would not survive in the world without her, may also dream of herself in this form. If so, it is a warning to her not to neglect her own needs.

## PRINCESS

The princess embodies the spontaneous, romantic, innocent young girl who longs to make the world a reflection of her inner idyll. The flip side of this character is the seductress who cynically uses her alluring qualities to beguile and corrupt. She usually appears in dreams as a mythical siren or a male erotic fantasy.

## AMAZON

It is a popular misconception that the Amazon symbolizes physical strength. As an archetype in dream symbolism, she represents superior feminine intellect. In a competitive context she will frequently appear in the guise of a huntress, representing in the dream the type of woman who confronts men to compensate for her own lack of confidence.

## PRIESTESS/WISE OLD MAN

The priestess personifies the quality of intuition. Her appearance in dreams indicates an awakening of the subtler, psychic senses or the need to attend to the needs of the inner self which may be overwhelmed by materialistic concerns.

Her dark side is the witch. As a dream symbol, she signifies a person wrapped up in their own fantasies and suspicious of the motives of others. Her appearance can suggest a fear of persecution, but as with the true witches of the past she may hold secrets which could be beneficial to the dreamer.

Male potential is embodied in the figure known as The Wise Old Man. He is likely to make his first appearance in a man's dreams from the age of 40, when most men begin to seriously consider the meaning of their lives and look to their own potential rather than to their father for inspiration and insight. The appearance of this figure in a dream is extremely significant, and any advice given in the dream should be considered very seriously indeed.

## THE FATHER

In his positive aspect the father represents respect for authority, protection, acceptable standards of behaviour and guidance. His dark side is the ogre, a strict disciplinarian who seeks to repress individuality and constrain the dreamer's uniqueness with rigid, irrational rules.

## THE YOUTH

The youth embodies enthusiasm for life, a healthy restlessness, a positive outlook, limitless potential, inquisitiveness and faith in the future.

The reverse of this aspect of the male self is the perpetual wanderer, who fears commitment and responsibility. He may also appear in the form of an explorer, adventurer or a hunter, any of which the dreamer may perceive as the appealing romantic aspect of himself, but which is instead more likely to imply that he is rash and self-centred.

## THE HERO

The hero is the embodiment of the male will. It personifies his courage, determination to succeed, fortitude and resolve. To dream of seeing ourselves as this figure, or of watching a heroic figure achieve something we would like to achieve in waking life, is to recognize the potential within. It also suggests that we have not acted on these instincts for fear of failure or of ridicule for displaying such overtly masculine attributes in front of others.

The reverse of this vital force is the villain or megalomaniac who, being in essence the ego without emotional stability, is obsessed by the desire to impose his will upon others and to demean them in the process. To dream of this figure is to be warned by the unconscious of a tendency to allow the ego to dominate the self and alienate others.

## THE MAGICIAN

The magician personifies intuition, imagination and mastery of the immutable forces of nature, an aspect of the self which many men have ignored to their cost. Harnessing this vital force is the key to wholeness as it balances against modern man's tendency to put all his energy into worldly activities at the expense of his inner development. It is not uncommon for an adolescent to dream of a struggle between a magician or witch and the other three male archetypes. This is an expression of the inner struggle between his sensual and spiritual selves, and should not be dismissed as fantasy.

## PEOPLE AND PROFESSIONS

We sometimes use contrasting characters in our dreams to personify our own conflicting emotions about something which concerns us. If we are wondering whether we should go to university or take a job, we might dream that we are watching a student sitting an exam or a busy executive making lots of money. Such dreams represent our hopes and anxieties about these choices, and do not necessarily reflect the reality of the situation, so they should not be seen as predicting how we will cope in the same situation. The people who take these roles in our dreams might be people we know who have already done these things, they might be people who play those parts in films, TV or even advertisements, or they might even be people

who lack the qualities we consider necessary to be successful in such situations.

Projecting our own characteristics onto imaginary or familiar individuals is a convenient way for us to consider them objectively, especially if we unconsciously consider them to be objectionable.

## ACTOR/ACTRESS

The dreamer is testing out the idea of introducing a previously hidden aspect of his or her personality to the world. The audience's reaction will show to what degree you, the dreamer, feel comfortable with this new persona. If no audience is present, it suggests that you are more at ease expressing this side of your nature in private.

If you are acting with other people it implies that you are not 'playing it straight' with others in your waking life or that you consider it necessary to put on 'a front' because other people do not appear to be showing their true nature.

## BISHOP

For the religious person, a bishop or church official of any kind symbolizes devotion, self-discipline and inner strength, characteristics which the dreamer unconsciously aspires to. For the non-believer, however, bishops and officials represent conformity, insular attitudes and perhaps even corruption.

## ARTIST/COMPOSER/POET

Any of these represents the creative impulse of the dreamer which may have been suppressed and is now demanding to be allowed to express itself. Such figures reveal hidden talent but do not, of course, predict whether others will recognize or appreciate it!

## CHILD

A child is usually representative of the dreamer's inner child, the child-like quality which views the world as a playground full of possibilities. Even if our own childhood was unhappy, this aspect of the self remains within as a personification of promise and potential. However, the child may also symbolize your own childhood, so if this figure appears in your dream, it might be revealing to recall what it was doing, what expression it bore, how it was dressed, who it was reacting to and what its surroundings were like.

## GNOME

The psychoanalyst C. G. Jung (see page 14) once invoked a 'waking dream' to find an answer to a series of disturbing visions. The first figure he met was a hideous dwarf whom he recognized as the guardian of his own unconscious mind, an archetypal figure common to us all who personifies the censoring mechanism. If one can

programme the mind to recognize this figure whenever it appears, it should be possible to induce a lucid dream, overcome the guardian and gain access to the unconscious at will.

Adherents of Freud also see the gnome or dwarf as a significant symbol, only they believe it represents the penis.

## CROWD OR MOB

A crowd usually appears in dreams as an irrational force opposed to the will and beliefs of the dreamer. It can represent the world at large, the community in which the dreamer lives and works or his or her own subconscious.

If you are jeered at by the mob in your dream, it indicates that your ideas on a particular subject have not been properly thought through. If you feel threatened by the anonymity of the crowd, this implies that you feel pressured to conform in waking life or fear criticism about your views or image in waking life.

To become part of the crowd can indicate a desire to be accepted, even at the cost of losing your own identity. More commonly, this dream can signify a need to escape responsibilities. In one of the more disturbing dreams of this type, the dreamer is caught up and carried along by a surging crowd. This symbolizes a fear of losing control and being swept along by the momentum of events.

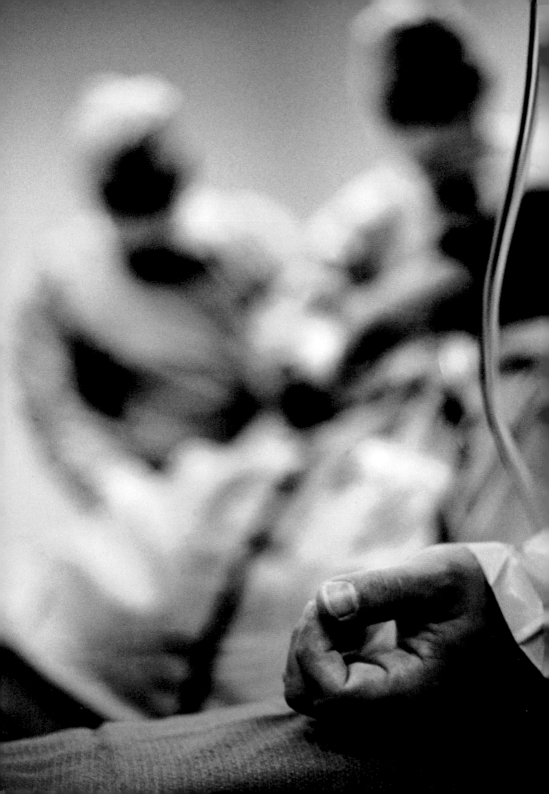

## DOCTOR/NURSE/ MEDICAL STAFF

Depending on the context and the emotions which such figures arouse in the dreamer, doctors and nurses can symbolize a fear of illness, authority, of being interrogated, or embarrassment concerning bodily functions. Alternatively, a dream featuring any of these figures may indicate a strong need to confide in someone or even the fear of being rescued.

## SHOP ASSISTANT/ OFFICE WORKER

Anonymous characters who are preoccupied with mundane tasks usually stand in for our dislike of repetition and our frustration with our lives as they seem at the present moment.

Dreaming of being stuck with meaningless, boring, repetitive tasks is an indication that we should be considering making radical changes in our lives, both at work and at home.

## TRIBAL PEOPLE AND OTHER CULTURES

These can represent anything uncommon and unknown to which the dreamer is attracted but at the same time fears. Primitive people generally symbolize repressed desires, invariably sexual. Eastern guru-type figures symbolize secret knowledge and medical problems. Indians symbolize spirituality. Native Americans

represent the secrets of Nature. If the theme of the dream is obscure, it can be taken that these images express a general fear of the unfamiliar.

## GIANT

Any giant figure in a dream signifies a threat to the dreamer's self-image, a deflater of the ego and a sense of being cut 'down to size'. If you appear as a child among giants in your dream, this can either be a recollection of the adults you knew at that time who you perceived to be giants, or people you know now in adulthood and perceive as being more 'grown up' than you are.

## AUTHORITY FIGURE

These are often substitutes for the dreamer's father although they can also symbolize the anonymous forces of the state. Teachers can appear to remind us how vulnerable we once felt and can still feel when challenged about something which we have not considered carefully enough. Judges and policemen can stand in for our own conscience concerning an act which we knew to be wrong when we committed it.

Respite dream will not be achieved until we acknowledge this wrong. If the dreamer thinks he has been unjustly criticized in the past by a parent or teacher, then an authority figure can appear as someone who is not to be trusted.

## MILITARY FIGURE

Any individual or group of figures representing the armed forces is symbolic of our attempt to constrain our aggressive impulses. The more active the characters are, the fiercer is the struggle between the aggressive impulse and the fear of losing control of emotions. A dream centring on the importance of rank or battle formations, indicates anxiety regarding orderliness in waking life and a desire that life should conform to our concept of right and wrong.

## JAILER

The jailer symbolizes the dreamer's conscience. He may appear intent on jailing the dreamer for what the dreamer considers to be uncontrollable impulses or for a past error that he or she has committed and for which punishment is unconsciously sought to resolve the sense of guilt.

## KING AND QUEEN/ EMPEROR AND EMPRESS

This pairing symbolizes the dreamer's parents. It can also symbolize cherished ideas or beliefs which we consider set us apart from other people and give real meaning or value to our lives.

## MONSTER

The embodiment of irrational fears. The fear of being afraid or of losing control of one's emotions often takes the form of a hideous creature. A fear of something tangible and real will take a recognizable form, albeit often disguised. By using a monster born entirely from the imagination the unconscious is in effect informing us that our fear of being afraid has no basis in reality. The monster may roar, pull a hideous face and bare its teeth, but if we confront it and demand to know what it is doing or wants the hideous image should break up and fade.

## YOUTHFULNESS

If the context of the dream indicates that the youth is not the male aspect of the self, embodying enthusiasm for life, then it is likely to be telling the dreamer to look for something of relevance from this period. Instead of presenting ourselves in this guise in the dream the unconscious may even use a youthful image of someone that we know well to make the same point. Perhaps the dreamer is struggling with feelings or a situation similar to one at an earlier age? If so, the unconscious could be hinting that the solution lies within the lessons of that previous experience.

## VAMPIRE

The vampire or succubus is an archetypal image. Even if your dream seems to have been triggered by watching a horror movie, do not initially disregard it

as meaningless. The appearance of this predatory being may be a projection of your guilt concerning sexual impulses, by literally creating an external focus to blame such feelings upon. Alternatively, it may be the destructive force of the anima, which is asserting its need for attention by sucking the vital force from you in dreams.

## SCIENTIST/PROFESSOR

This character represents the rational self. This figure usually appears when we are considering something of importance and need the outcome demonstrated to our satisfaction before we will commit ourselves. It is important to understand that these characters will only present one side of the argument and will not necessarily provide the 'right' or only solution.

## ROCK OR MOVIE STAR/CELEBRITY

A glamorous celebrity is usually the embodiment of the anima/animus as idealized by the unconscious. A man might dream of a strong-willed woman, for example, if he admires that characteristic in his own feminine side. A woman might dream of a considerate man if that is the most admirable quality among her masculine attributes.

## PURSUER

Any character who threatens us in a dream is likely to symbolize

our Shadow (see page 64). Although the appearance of the pursuer or intruder may be disturbing, it is important to realize that it symbolizes an aspect of the personality which has been denied and is literally haunting the dreamer in the hope of being recognized and integrated into the personality.

The best way to achieve this is to programme the mind each night before going to sleep by repeating to yourself that when the pursuer appears you will stop, face it and ask it what it wants of you. This move almost always guarantees a revealing answer and puts a stop to the nightmares.

## SPORTSMEN/WOMEN

Sports personalities embody the competitive urge. Dreaming that you are a spectator at a sports event or are participating in a sport could be compensation for a sedentary lifestyle. Through such dreams the unconscious could be prompting you to be more active by reminding you of the feeling of exhilaration that comes with activity and the sense of satisfaction which accompanies achievement in any discipline. If, however, in your dream you are participating in a sport with which you feel uncomfortable or you are losing a game, this can be an indication of a sense of low self-esteem, a fear of experiencing failure within a competitive context in waking life (for example in the workplace) or of being humiliated in front of other people.

## FAMILIES

Our experience of family life serves as the model for our future relationships. In dreams each member of the family, past and present, can represent the dreamer's ideal of what a good father, mother, sister, brother, son or daughter should be. Alternatively, the dreamer may unconsciously identify a characteristic with a particular family member. A lazy brother, for example, might be substituted for the dreamer's prospective partner, suggesting that the dreamer fears that the partner will be as lazy as the brother.

Fathers frequently appear as authority figures and mothers as sources of comfort and security. Brothers can symbolize the youth/wanderer or hero/villain aspect of the male personality, and sisters may represent the princess/seductress or amazon/huntress aspect of the female. The unconscious may even use imagery as a pun, using the dreamer's real brother or sister to warn of a tendency to be as solitary, chaste and unworldly as a monk or nun.

Brothers can represent the masculine qualities of the female dreamer and may also substitute for a woman's male partner, a man's best friend, or any male figure for whom the dreamer

feels an affinity. In dreams a man's brother can also symbolize his Shadow.

Sisters can stand in for female friends or partners, but they are more likely to reflect the feminine qualities of the male dreamer.

Grandparents can often appear as manifestations of the Wise Old Man and Great Mother, symbolizing the dreamer's innate potential for self-actualization and maturity. However, if the dreamer's grandparents have not coped well in old age, they can appear in dreams as symbols of frailty, helplessness and the dreamer's own fear of death.

To dream of a contented family is an indication that we are happy in ourselves, that we have achieved a balance of qualities which are normally represented by different members of the traditional family unit and that we feel secure in our own situation. To dream of an acrimonious family indicates that we feel fragmented and 'out of sorts' at the present time.

To dream that a family member interrupts a sexual act between you and your partner suggests that you are struggling to become independent and are anxious to gain either approval or permission from that particular family member (usually a parent) to grow up.

The death of parents symbolizes guilt at wanting independence. If the dreamer causes the death of the parent it

can express frustration at not being entirely independent. Alternatively, the dream can serve as a release for the conflicting, intense emotions which are a normal part of every family life.

## ANIMALS

From the earliest times man has noted that the animal kingdom is a fragmented reflection of his own qualities, impulses, natural instincts and characteristics. Primitive cultures considered certain species to be possessed by spirits that they believed they could harness if they killed the animal and wore its skin. Today psychologists interpret the actions and appearance of animals in our dreams as personifications of these same instincts, impulses, qualities and characteristics.

Different species of animals symbolize specific qualities and the appearance of an animal in our dreams signifies that the animal principle within us is craving attention. This usually manifests itself as vitality, instinct, cunning, curiosity, sociability, mobility and moodiness and does not necessarily indicate our 'bestial' passions.

To dream of an injured animal suggests that we feel guilty about denying our animal impulses. These 'animal impulses' should not be automatically read as being sexual in nature, and it could merely be a difficulty in showing feelings, perhaps because of self-consciousness or fear of rejection. The injured animal featured in the dream might represent an elderly or sick relation to whom the dreamer finds difficulty in expressing his or her feelings. A 'dumb' animal is usually a safer focus for the dreamer's compassion.

If young animals appear in your dream, you are playing with the idea of having a family of your own by testing your maternal or paternal instincts in a 'safe' non-committal way; that is, without facing the image of human children and the responsibilities that they imply.

Dreams in which we stalk, hunt or kill an animal are concerned with our desire to control our own animal instincts which we acknowledge as being vital components of our personality. However, if in the dream we are the pursued, the implication is fear of these instincts. Such dreams should be resolved by re-entering the dream on waking and imagining a positive end in which the animal is tamed or befriended.

Dreams which culminate in the dreamer taming the animal are more promising than those in which the animal is killed. The former resolution indicates that the animal instincts have been acknowledged and integrated, while the latter indicates a fear so great that feelings have to be repressed completely by annihilating them. However, if the animal in the dream is either skinned or eaten after being killed, the indication is that its vital force has been absorbed into the dreamer's psyche.

## BAT

In Western cultures the bat has long been perceived as a symbol of the forces of darkness because of its association with night. However, the Chinese have traditionally associated bats with good fortune, namely wealth, good health and a long life. If your dream features one of these winged creatures, consider the context carefully to find out whether it is simply a warning against watching too many horror movies or is a sign of something serious.

## DOMESTIC PETS

In addition to the specific significance of dogs (see page 74) and cats (see page 75), pets in general can be seen as symbolic of domestic contentment. Through such dreams the unconscious is saying that you have a sense of well-being synonymous with a comfortable, secure, well-kept home and that you are comfortable sharing space with your natural instincts. Goldfish, for example, are considered symbols of wealth by the Chinese. To dream of goldfish in an aquarium is better still as analysts consider the water, which is symbolic of the emotions, to represent the love surrounding the dreamer.

## BEAR

Bears are a symbol of brute force and are therefore most likely to refer to an overbearing father, or father figure (for example a teacher or a boss). Dreaming that you are being hugged by a bear to the point of breathlessness is suggestive of the influence of an overbearing mother.

In the Middle Ages orthodox Christianity used the bear to symbolize cruelty and greed. More recently Christian missionaries used it to symbolize the heathens who needed licking in to shape by the 'parent'. Jung considered the bear to represent the uncontrollable aspects of the unconscious. Certain Native American tribes and the Chinese perceive it as a symbol of courage. The Chinese also say that dreaming of a bear is a sign that the dreamer will be blessed with sons.

## MONKEY

Small monkeys represent the playful side of our nature, but at the same time the infuriatingly infantile aspect. To dream of small mischievous monkeys is to recognize that the immature aspects of ourselves, which until then we had considered to be charming, might be seen by others as childish and irritating.

In contrast, in dreams gorillas can be seen as representing the unfamiliar and unpredictable aspects of the personality, or of future events.

## ELEPHANT

Elephants have traditionally been seen as animals that never forget. A white elephant is a tag used to symbolize expensive mistakes. In the hidden language of dreams, elephants symbolize longevity and a dogged determination on the part of the dreamer to succeed despite the formidable obstacles in the way. Dreaming about them acknowledges that our progress may be ponderously slow and we may not impress others with our dynamism or radical new ideas, but we are sure to win in the end.

## DOLPHIN

Dolphins are supremely intelligent and gentle creatures and as such have been adopted by the New Age movement as symbols of spirituality. To dream of a dolphin indicates the quality of inner calm and contentment and an affinity with all the aspects of one's being.

## BIRD

Birds are universal symbols personifying the freedom of flight and high aspirations. However, to dream of flight is not merely to desire freedom from life's responsibilities and limitations, but can be an actual sensory experience of leaving the limitations of the body during sleep (see Lucid dreaming, page 28–29). Certain birds, such as doves, have special symbolic significance. All birds of prey

convey either the dreamer's predatory instincts or fear of being devoured by over-ambitious rivals.

## DOG

Dogs are considered faithful, but also tenacious and so, depending on the context of the dream, they can either symbolize loyalty, as in the phrase 'a man's best friend', or the habit of worrying at a problem rather than resolving it rationally. A dream featuring a dog could even indicate that you are relishing the prospect of a project that you can get your teeth into.

## BULL

As with most animal archetypes there is a negative and a positive aspect to the bull. If the dream is disturbing the bull indicates unfettered anger and an urge to destroy whatever it is intending to charge in the dream. In a peaceful dream it stands for power and the vital forces, specifically male virility and female fertility.

## HORSE

A stallion is symbolic of male virility and energy, while mares represent the female. Dreaming that one has mastered the animal and is enjoying a pleasant ride is indicative of harnessing that vital force. However, struggling to master a horse of the opposite sex to the rider suggests a secret desire to possess the person whom that horse represents. If it

is not obvious to the dreamer who that person might be, it could be worthwhile recalling any clues that might have been evident on the livery or in the surroundings. Nowadays that other male symbol of power, the car, has all but replaced the horse in dreamlore.

## COW

Cows were an ancient symbol of the mother and by extension Mother Earth, or the regenerative power of nature. To Buddhists and Hindus the cow is a symbol of patience. In other cultures the cow is revered as a symbol of happiness. To dream of a cow, particularly a white cow, is said to be very auspicious. Contemporary dream analysts would probably disagree and prefer to see it as a sign that the dreamer is in danger of becoming too docile.

## GOAT

Goats may have an innocent association for the dreamer, but in the Judeo-Christian tradition they are associated with rampant sexual impulses and the Devil. Dreams can draw on this symbol if the dreamer has a strong religious belief. If not the more likely associations are with sure-footedness, male virility and female fertility.

## FOX

The fox symbolizes the wily, cunning trickster who waits for nightfall to embark on his predatory rounds. The dreamer has to be especially careful in attributing these characteristics appropriately. You may think your dream is pinpointing ambitious colleagues or a partner who is having an affair on the sly. However, it is just as likely your unconscious is using the fox to warn you against your own suspicious nature!

## HARE/RABBIT

The hare is traditionally associated with the moon, with natural magic and regeneration, but it can also represent the animal's own attributes of swiftness and prolific procreation. Christianity appropriated it as a symbol of self-sacrifice and so it may well appear in a dream as a symbol of something that needs to be sacrificed before the dreamer can move on.

## INSECT

A dream in which insects appear signififes the fear of being overwhelmed by something beyond the dreamer's control. It is the size and speed of tiny insects which is potentially disturbing to our psyche together with their alien appearance which we internalize as fear of the invasive and unpredictable.

Most of us have a horror of parasites, particularly those associated with decomposing corpses. We transfer these fears of our own mortality and vulnerability to often harmless insects in our dreams. In rare cases dreaming of parasitic insects can indicate a fear of being burdened with unwanted children. Spiders, too, have a specific symbolic significance: both our fear of the unknown and the overpowering female, usually representative of a mother. A large predatory spider can represent a dominating woman by whom the dreamer fears being drained of vitality and then devoured.

## SNAKE

The traditional symbol of evil and sexuality, which has led most analysts to attribute negative sexual connotations to its appearance in dreams. It is certainly a potent and recurrent phallic symbol. However, the most significant attribute of the snake is that it periodically sheds its skin, making it more appropriate as a symbol of change and renewal.

## DOVE

Doves have been universal symbols of peace since ancient times, although by nature they are fretful creatures. In pagan Pompeii and a number of pre-Christian cults they were symbols of sexual union and childbirth. The dove's many appearances in the bible as a divine messenger means that to see one in a dream is to hope for selfless, lasting love in waking life.

## CAT/LION

Because of their association with witchcraft, cats have remained a symbol of ill-omen. Witches were believed to keep a black cat as a 'familiar' to help them communicate with the devil. In some cultures domestic cats are seen as symbols of sensuality and the feline instincts. In dreamlore lions, panthers and the other big cats personify stealth, capriciousness, indolence and vindictiveness, none of which are exclusively female attributes!

# Significant Objects

IN OUR DREAMS everyday objects can assume a symbolic significance. We unconsciously project our disappointments, frustrations, fears and even our sexual desires onto the most mundane items, but on waking we tend to dismiss them as mere props in a surreal fantasy. But in the dreamworld nothing is insignificant, nothing appears arbitrarily or without purpose. Containers can hold secrets, keys can unlock memories of long forgotten places and people, treasured possessions can reveal our insecurities and mementoes can evoke emotions which lie dormant during the waking hours. In the dreamworld machines can be substitutes for our bodies and minds, so that if we dream of them breaking down it might be a warning to slow down before physical ailments and stress-related disorders force us to take a break. The number of objects, their colour and even their condition can add to the strength of the signal breaking through from the unconscious and also add to our knowledge of who we are and what we really value in life.

## SEXUAL SYMBOLS

Any long, pointed object which can penetrate another or is capable of emitting liquid under pressure could be a phallic symbol. For that reason certain tools, weapons, gardening equipment and farming implements could be used by the unconscious as obscure symbols of the male genitalia. Even such innocuous objects as umbrellas, bottles, certain musical instruments, water pistols, hoses and syringes could have sexual connotations in the dreamscape. Milk and other liquids may appear as symbols of semen, although dreaming of watching helplessly as a precious fluid drains away through a crack in the ground could simply be expressing a fear of losing one's vitality or of regretting past mistakes (hence the saying 'crying over spilt milk'). Playing with a ball could reflect curiosity regarding male masturbation, although for men it could also have an entirely 'innocent' meaning in recalling the leisure and simple pleasures of childhood. Hollow objects and containers often symbolize the vagina or the womb.

## ALCOHOL

To dream of shopping for alcohol or consuming large quantities of liquor could indicate a desire to erase a disturbing memory, or symbolize the craving for someone whose presence we find intoxicating and refreshing at the same time. If the image is a symbol of passion the relationship is likely to be superficial, based solely on physical attraction and may be potentially destructive.

It could also be a substitute image for our desire to be able to 'loosen up' and share the pleasures that we imagine other people enjoy when we let go and lose our inhibitions.

## BOOKS

In waking life we associate books with knowledge, but in the dreamworld they symbolize our memories. Books bound in leather and elaborately embossed symbolize treasured memories, but could also imply a certain nostalgia and sentimentality which might be misplaced. Well-thumbed paperbacks which are yellowing, curling at the edges and cracked at the spine are symbolic of a hard life in which there has been little time for dwelling on the past. In this case memories are merely data banks of useful facts and experience and the dream is signifying that the answer to whatever troubles us at present or in the future is to be found in our past.

## CRACKED OR BROKEN OBJECTS

These are often connected with the suspicion that life is not all that it could be, that we have been let down, ill-used or fobbed off with shoddy goods or an unsatisfactory explanation. It can also imply that we do not believe that we have what we need to fulfil our present needs or future ambitions. If the damaged object is a container in which we need to carry something crucial, such as water to put out a fire or sand to help build a house, it indicates the feeling that time is running out for something we are desperate to complete and possibly the fear that our efforts are being undermined by less conscientious people.

## WEAPONS

As in waking life, weapons can be used as instruments of attack or defence in dreams and therefore it is important to establish the context in which they are used, how they are used and against whom they are used. Generally, weapons can be seen as extensions of the male force to subdue or to stand firm against a threatening force. It is not uncommon for both men and women to dream of fighting a formidable and strangely familiar figure which analysis later 'proves' was representative of the dreamer's Shadow. At other times the antagonist may be the dreamer's partner, whom the dreamer feels cannot be impressed or convinced through words alone. If it is a partner, the use of guns, swords, knives,

arrows and pikes could reflect the belief that the cause of the conflict is sexual and that one partner is resisting the dominance of the other.

## MONEY, TREASURE AND VALUABLE ITEMS

Most of us believe that if we have enough money we can somehow protect ourselves from everything that we see as being negative in life, even though we know that this is irrational and untrue. In our dreams we equate health, social status and even our sexual potency with the amount of money we possess or desire. Not having enough money symbolizes a fear of losing face, influence or power, while winning large amounts of cash symbolizes a need for respect and security and perhaps also an unconscious desire to be recognized and acknowledged as being superior to our neighbours or colleagues.

If we have recently endured emotional upsets or ill-health we may dream of receiving an unexpected windfall to make everything right again and to cushion us from the effects of any future shocks. To dream of bargaining, arguing about money or profiting from financial deals is often a reflection of a need to outwit someone we know in waking life who we believe is more fortunate, more talented, more intelligent or is better educated than we are. Such dreams indicate an inferiority complex and immaturity which is expressed in the need to flaunt wealth as if it was proof of personal value. Such dreams reveal an unconscious desire to impress others and at the same time to convince ourselves that we do not need the attributes that our 'rivals' possess in order to have value. Underlining such images is the compulsion to 'get away with something', because we do not trust enough in our innate qualities to make a favourable impression.

Dreaming of being forced to give away or spend large amounts of money to settle debts implies a guilt complex and the need 'to pay' for what we have done to restore the balance. Hoarding money has the same implications as it does in real life – a distrust of others, a fear of the future and of having to rely on our own resources. On an unconscious level it also symbolizes a profound fear of rejection, as the unconscious often equates love, the most precious thing one can give, with valuable commodities in the material world. To dream of going on a spending spree is therefore expressing a desire to shake off inhibitions and indulge the senses and live life to the full, regardless of whether or not our affections are returned.

## TOYS

Teddy bears and other mementoes of childhood reflect a desire to return to the imagined idyll of our formative years and a time when people, life and values appeared to be simple, consistent and predictable. Toy guns, military vehicles and soldiers symbolize the dreamer's distrust of his own aggressive masculine nature, or animus if the dreamer is female. These toys indicate that the dreamer is 'playing' with the traditional concepts of masculinity, testing them out on imaginary playmates in a harmless way. It could be that the dream is reflecting a conflict between the dreamer and the aggressive masculine aspect of their (male or female) partner, in which case the context should make the meaning clear.

Dolls and puppets can also have a special significance, representing people from our past whose identity might be found in significant details, even if the features of the dolls are not immediately familiar. A female, for example, might be represented by a doll with the same hair colour or style of clothing because it was once remarked that she was as pretty as a little doll. A man thought of as being stiff and formal might be symbolized by a toy soldier and so on. Of importance is what we do to them in the dream and what, if anything, we say to them. We will probably act as a child in the dream, confiding our true feelings in our toys just as we did in childhood. Although it may sound sinister, we may need to act out a confrontation with that person or release aggression. Dreams of childhood can make a harmless, but effective, setting in which to do so.

## KEYS

Keys are symbols of the solution to a problem, the nature of which should be obvious from the context and details of the dream. What is needed is to follow the dream through to see what the key will open. If this does not happen in the dream itself, simply re-enter the dream as soon as possible upon waking and allow the events to unfold effortlessly as if it was a daydream. If the key fits a door, it suggests the solution lies in a change of circumstance, although the nature of the room you enter could give further clues. If it fits the lock of a box or chest the solution could lie in something which has been suppressed or simply forgotten. Again, the symbolic significance of the furniture should give further clues. If the key fits a piano, Freudian analysts would probably insist that the dream has sexual significance and that the dreamer wishes to 'perform' with someone they want to make 'beautiful music with' or

who they seek to dominate. Alternatively, it could be that he or she simply wants to develop a talent which has been neglected for some time. However, it might also be that the problem being pondered has no simple answer and so the piano keys will symbolize the innumerable variations and possibilities with which the dreamer can play around in search of harmony in his or her life. If the dream does not resolve itself satisfactorily, it might be important to recall where the key was found If, for example, it was found under a bed, it could signify that the dreamer needs rest and relaxation. If it was discovered in a garden under a bush, it could signify that the dreamer needs a period of reflection in a quiet and inspiring spot.

## MACHINES

Heavy machines with moving parts invariably represent the body, specifically the stomach. Complex electronic devices such as computers frequently symbolize the human brain. It may be that warnings of impending physical problems first appear in dreams as images of overloaded or rusting machinery before the first symptoms are felt.

Stress or intense mental fatigue could be reflected in dreams centring on fused or temperamental electrical devices. If the dream reflects

anxiety over a particular problem, it could be useful to re-enter it and ask the computer which solution it recommends, or what the consequences of taking various forms of action would be.

If you find yourself operating machinery which is carrying out monotonous tasks, a possible interpretation might be that life has become routine and predictable. In such cases the unconscious is warning that you are living life 'mechanically', motivated by habit rather than curiosity, ambition or emotion.

# Significant Situations

IN OUR DREAMS we often live out our fantasies and confront our fears. But not all our fears are well founded and not all our fantasies are unrealistic.

We are all familiar with the nightmares in which we find ourselves trapped or chased and we can readily believe that these reflect our general anxieties about life. But dreams are not simply about forcing us to face what we do not wish to acknowledge, or processing random thoughts while the mind is idle.

The purpose of dreams is to show us aspects of our personality that we have not yet acknowledged and abilities that we have not developed to the full. In our dreams we act according to our true nature, not the image we project to the outside world, but even the most sensitive person cannot be fully aware of all the facets of their own personality. Sleep serves as an opportunity for the unconscious to take centre stage and awaken us to the other roles we are qualified to play.

## ABANDONMENT

Dreams of being abandoned are common in childhood and often have no greater significance than as an expression of the child's desire to have a secure and happy home life. Sometimes the unconscious is playing with the idea of independence to test the strength of the attachment, as it does when imagining the death of a parent.

A clue to the true meaning of such dreams can often be found in the chosen location. If the child is abandoned in familiar surroundings close to its home it is confirming its need for the parent within safe boundaries. If it finds itself abandoned in a strange location, in a supermarket for example, it is the expression of a real anxiety that the parents might not be giving it their full attention.

## BEING CAUGHT OR TRAPPED

Dreaming of being entangled or ensnared in ropes and cables, is symbolic of the dreamer's fear of being restricted from doing whatever he or she wants to do. It can also express a real fear of being overwhelmed by unexpected commitments, most commonly financial or family-related ones because these are the ones from which we have the most trouble freeing ourselves.

Dreaming of being trapped by falling rubble or trees suggests that emotional or other pressures are threatening to 'get on top' of you and pin you down. The best way to exorcise such anxieties is to face the facts during daylight and accept the consequences of whichever option you decide upon.

Being locked in a room is a more complex case because it is necessary to discover what led you to the location and who locked you in. Being imprisoned can be symbolic of a sense of being cut off from the outside world, from society, the family or peer group. Discovering who imprisoned you can, therefore, give a valuable clue to the cause of the dream.

In recalling the events or in re-entering the dream on waking to resolve it, you may discover that you entrapped yourself, through a craving for something which you secretly desire but which you know is not good for you.

## NAKEDNESS

If being undressed in your dream is a pleasurable sensation it suggests that you regard social conventions as artificial and are making a show of shedding your inhibitions. You may also consider the other people in the scene to be hypocritical in their conventional attitudes and want to shock them. If, however, you are embarrassed by being naked, in your dream, whether you are alone or before others, then you are likely to be manifesting a fear of being seen to be inadequate or looking foolish.

The question is whether we believe it is our 'real self' which is being exposed as inadequate, or the persona, the façade that we hide behind. If the latter, then perhaps the unconscious is encouraging us to drop our pretence and expose our true nature to the world in confidence. This is likely if we have been overly defensive or secretive and are beginning to realize that this is causing us more problems than it solves. Such dreams may also occur if we are harbouring any guilt and are unconsciously seeking to unburden ourselves and 'come clean'.

The reactions of others can be equally significant. For example, if we find ourselves naked in a public place and no one appears to notice us, it could signify that we are too self-conscious and the dream is a compensatory reaction. But if the onlookers point and jeer, it betrays a fear of being rejected after trusting others with our true feelings.

In rare cases the image of seeing oneself naked may even be symbolic of the sensation of freedom which we feel on leaving the physical body, albeit briefly and unconsciously, during sleep as consciousness views the body as a second skin or overcoat.

## TAKING AN EXAM

This is one of the most common anxiety dreams and one which has been frequently dismissed as being merely a fear of returning to the constraints and pressures of school days. The more likely explanation for such dreams is that we are having doubts about our current career or a relationship and so our unconscious is revisiting a time when we faced equal anxiety as a means of reassurance. The purpose of this may be to remind the conscious mind that we overcame our fear to pass this earlier test, or, if we failed the exam, then at least such traumas are long gone just as this current problem will be in time.

To dream of sitting an exam that one is unprepared for is indicative of an unconscious anxiety concerning the overall course of one's life. It is as if the unconscious is rehearsing for the final judgement, regardless of whether or not the dreamer has a conscious belief in the hereafter.

## JOB INTERVIEW OR AUDITION

Although dreams of being tongue-tied during an audition or late for an important interview are more common among people who are constantly being tested in a competitive profession, they can also haunt us at times when we feel that we are losing control of life. Through such dreams the unconscious is warning of what might happen if we continue to drive ourselves too hard or take on too many commitments.

Dreams of this kind can be the result of our irrational need to explain past failures as being entirely our fault and may be stimulated by the memory of minor mistakes for which we are still punishing ourselves.

## WINNING

When we awake after dreaming of winning something or being awarded a prize we are often extremely disappointed to discover that it has only been a dream. We probably feel that the unconscious is teasing us with images of unrealistic achievements and by doing so is also emphasizing the crushing ordinariness of our waking lives. However, the unconscious does not work against us in this way.

A dream of succeeding at something should be seen as a message from the unconscious that we are not giving ourselves sufficient credit for the things we have achieved in life. If we do not recognize these smaller successes as something to be proud of then the unconscious has to present them to us in symbolic terms that we will understand.

## MAJOR DISASTER

Witnessing a major disaster or being caught up in a catastrophe is the unconscious mind's method of reminding us that we cannot cruise through life nor can we rely on everything to remain the way that we would like it to be. The more insular and entrenched we become in our own private world the more violently the real world will eventually force itself upon us and the more havoc it will wreak in our psyche when change comes. Such dreams are impressing on us the idea that the only thing we can truly rely upon is change.

## PURSUIT

It cannot be assumed that whatever is pursuing us in our dreams is intent on harming us or that we are the helpless victims of monsters from the unconscious. It may well be that we are running from responsibilities which we once took on quite willingly, but which we now realize are preventing us from pursuing our own self-interest. Even if we recognize our pursuer, it may only be standing in as the acceptable face of whatever is really troubling us. The real culprit is more than likely to be the everyday pressures and problems that we have unconsciously agreed to take on in order to evolve as personalities.

If we are pursuing something or somebody it could be that we still have an unresolved desire for, or attachment to, something which we cannot accept is beyond our comprehension or attainment. If we re-enter the dream on waking we may finally catch up with this elusive person or object and discover that it is something we no longer need and have only been pursuing out of a long-established habit. It is not unknown for the dreamer to find that what is being evaded is an aspect of him- or herself, the Shadow, or something which is desired but if obtained may be impossible to cope with.

## VIOLENT ARGUMENT OR FIGHT

A conflict of interests or a difficult decision can often manifest in dreams as a physical battle between two people who symbolize opposing views or impulses. In certain circumstances our 'opponent' might resemble someone we know in waking life because that person represents an aspect of ourselves with which we are unconsciously at war (see Serial Dreams, page 23).

It is also possible that dreams of violence might be compensating for repressed anger and resentment.

## PARALYSIS

There is a phase of sleep in which the body becomes almost rigid and it is this physical sensation which is often symbolized in dreams of immobility. If the stimulus for the dream is psychological, one interpretation could be indecision, or conflicting emotions, such as the fear of wanting something or someone which another aspect of the personality considers undesirable. The libido might desire to begin an extra-marital relationship while the conscience is 'freeze-framing' the action to bring the dreamer's attention to the possible

consequences. Alternatively, the dreamer might wish to escape from an addiction (which may be something comparatively harmless such as fattening foods or shopping) which the unconscious considers harmful but is unable to control because of the individual's secret craving.

Dreaming of being paralyzed can also symbolize the lack of confidence needed to move on in life. In such dreams we are aware that we cannot go back to the way things were, but neither have we the confidence to take the first steps towards change. If you suspect that this might be the explanation, try this technique. Upon waking, re-enter the dream and imagine you are growing to gigantic proportions so that you can look over the cityscape or mountains and see what awaits you on the other side. It may be a pleasant surprise.

## BEING EATEN

This is a rare but disturbing dream which usually ends before the jaws close upon us. The theme of the nightmare is the fear of being swallowed and not the threat of physical pain. The size of the monster's jaws is significant because these symbolize the fear we all share of being devoured by emptiness. It is the ego's fear of dying rather than a real fear of having consciousness extinguished. The Higher Self knows that consciousness continues beyond physical death,

but the ego does not share this knowledge. For this reason it is a more common dream among those who are preoccupied with material matters and whose egos therefore predominate.

## WEDDING

Wedding dreams are less likely to be precognitive than merely wish-fulfilment fantasies or symbols of a commitment to something of significance in our lives. This something is not necessarily a relationship. The image is being used by the unconscious to reinforce the seriousness of the situation and our responsibility to the enterprise. If the wedding makes the dreamer anxious, it could be reflecting an anxiety about making a commitment.

In rare cases wedding dreams can symbolize the integration of two complementary aspects of the dreamer's own personality such as his or her practical and creative qualities.

## DIVORCE

As with dreams of marriage the theme of divorce can be stimulated by a desire to break free from an attachment or commitment which is not necessarily connected with a personal relationship. We may be frustrated with a situation in waking life and putting all our energy into something which the unconscious is suggesting might be better left alone.

Such dreams may even occur to single people who are considering making a commitment to something or somebody. In effect, the individual is acting out in the safety of the imagination how he or she would cope with failure.

## PARTY

If the dreamer organizes the party and no one comes it suggests a fear of being a social outcast. If the party is a great success the imagery reflects a sense of well-being. Dreaming of hosting a successful party can have its negative aspect, because it might be the wish-fulfilment fantasy of someone who is too shy to risk rejection in waking life. The unconscious might be encouraging us to be more outgoing if it fears that the personality is being stifled by an irrational fear of rejection.

If the guests take over the party and we are sidelined it indicates a fear of losing control, though the most significant element may be what occurred during the party and what, if any, conversation can be recalled.

If we are a guest at the party, it might imply that we feel we are never at the centre of things, that we fail to receive our fair share of attention or that we believe we lack the confidence to stand out from the crowd.

Birthday and retirement parties can have a special significance in conveying the idea that a new era

has begun for the dreamer. Anniversary celebrations serve as reminders of significant events in the past which have a bearing on present circumstances.

## LOSING SOMETHING

Losing something in a dream suggests that we are either placing too much importance on material things or that we are going through a difficult period and are seeking a meaning in life. Perhaps, however, losing the item has resulted in a sense of relief, in which case we might unconsciously wish to be rid of whatever responsibilities or memories that object symbolizes for us. Further clues might be obtained from recalling the location, the colour and the number of the object or objects.

## POVERTY

One of the most common anxiety dreams is of losing all that we currently possess and being reduced to a life of extreme poverty. The dream usually starts at the point where we find ourselves homeless and in rags with no recollection of how we got into such a state. We are frequently confused and have a vague notion that whatever injustice has been done to us will be righted and our status and possessions restored as soon as we can convince the authorities of our true identity.

For people who measure their success by their professional

status and material wealth, the loss of all worldly possessions and self-esteem is the ultimate punishment. That is the primary purpose of the dream. The conscience has been unable to get through to the conscious mind and so it is seeking to bring some guilty secret to the dreamer's attention in a particularly graphic form. A similar scenario might be used when we feel that we have suffered an injustice and cannot let it rest. In this case the dream is symbolic of self-martyrdom, a visual appeal for the dreamer's suffering to be acknowledged.

## LOOKING FOR A LAVATORY

In the dreamworld the physical sensation of having a full bladder is typically translated into a search for a toilet. A more serious interpretation would suggest that we are seeking a private place where we can relieve ourselves of pent-up emotions. The implication here is that we feel unable to express our emotions to others.

A variation of this dream has the dreamer going to the toilet in full view of strangers. If these people show disapproval it indicates the dreamer is self-conscious and overly concerned with the opinion of others. If the strangers are unconcerned, it indicates that the dreamer has no such inhibitions in displaying inner feelings to others.

# Transport and Travel

TRAVEL IS ONE of the most significant recurring themes in our dreams. The journey is often symbolic of our progress in life and our expectations of what lies ahead. The vehicle we choose to travel in can reveal much about our state of mind, our emotional make-up, our physical fitness and even our health.

Setting off on a journey is symbolic of a new beginning which we are about to make in waking life, but the attitude you have towards the journey in the dream might be more important than the destination. So consider if you are excited or anxious about the prospect of venturing into new territory.

## PREPARATIONS FOR TRAVEL

In a dream the preparations we make for a long journey say a lot about our temperament, character and also our bad habits! If we dream of setting out without many provisions, maps or, as is often the case in dreams, of much sense of purpose or destination, it indicates a rather casual attitude to life. That may well be a good thing, in that it reveals that we do not impose too many expectations on ourselves, but take things as they come. Perhaps we cope better with problems as they arise rather than worrying too much about what might lie around the corner or waste energy considering the implications of our every action. But it is not so good if the image is suggesting that we are so carefree and unconcerned with reality that it does not take much to throw us off course, or that we will drift with events without a sense of purpose or of our roots.

## PROVISIONS

A lack of provisions is indicative of a positive personality and suggests that we think that life will provide for us. On the other hand this feature can also be indicative of a dangerous naivety. Perhaps life has been pretty supportive so far, but it is not realistic to always trust in providence or other people to bail us out when we need it. To dream of carrying a spare tyre, tools, maps and provisions indicates a practical, realistic attitude, although if these appear unduly important it can be suggestive of an intense, overly formal nature and entrenched habits which might be making every family holiday as much fun as being on army manoeuvres! So beware. If there is a great emphasis in the dream on packing bags and loading up with possessions the implication is that the dreamer has difficulty leaving the past behind or of truly relaxing and letting go of commitments and concerns.

Luggage can also symbolize responsibilities, either real or imagined. We tend to either ignore our responsibilities and hope they will go away or exaggerate them and be a martyr to them to show how 'mature' we are in taking them on. If you dream of driving off without the luggage or of struggling under the weight of baggage that is bursting at the seams, then you will know which of these character types you unconsciously consider yourself to be!

## ROADS

In general, natural paths and tracks represent the landscape of an inner journey, whereas man-made streets symbolize the road ahead in waking life.

Winding country lanes can indicate a need for relaxation, to 'stretch one's legs' to escape an intense situation. Alternatively, the scene might reflect deep satisfaction to have reached the psychological equivalent of open country after a period when one has been restricted and under stress. The context and atmosphere should make the meaning obvious. If there is a feeling of being lost in an unfamiliar landscape it could still be a positive image, because the unconscious might be suggesting that it is time to stop trying to exercise control on every aspect of one's life and instead explore new territory.

Being stuck behind a tractor is a common dream experienced by compulsively ambitious people who literally drive themselves to distraction when they could be enjoying pleasant things around them.

Town and city streets generally appear in dreams when the dreamer's life is complicated and the way ahead in not clear. The maze of criss-crossing, interconnecting streets and jungle of signs and lights symbolizes inner conflict and confusion. Dreams of driving in the city are often indicative of indecision and being faced with an overwhelming number of choices. City and town driving is a series of starts and stops, of giving way and being alert to the impulsive actions of others.

That is why the setting is useful to the unconscious for preparing us for the unpredictable.

Cul-de-sacs symbolize the end of a phase in one's life, a dead-end. A fork in the road can indicate a parting of the ways from someone who has come a long way on the journey of life with the driver/dreamer.

A fast-flowing, motorway indicates a life of broad horizons and a choice of fulfilling opportunities. The image also suggests that it will be a long journey before the ultimate goal is reached and that this is not necessarily known to the dreamer. It may be just a vague ambition to be successful, to 'get somewhere' in life, without an idea of precisely what area of activity to put the effort into. But the journey itself should be smooth with few obstacles and unnecessary diversions.

If the dream journey is set on a busy motorway and we are hemmed in on all sides the implication is that we are under stress in waking life and being forced to follow the dictates of others, to run with the pack rather than risk asserting our individuality. In such cases we may find ourselves gazing across to the fields or houses beyond the crash barrier. The view seen here should reveal a lot about what we would really like to be doing with our lives and where we should consider redirecting our efforts.

If we dream of being stuck on a motorway with the view ahead obscured by other cars it suggests that we are stagnating in a particular situation in waking life, perhaps an unfulfilling job with little prospect of promotion or a soul-destroying occupation with too many people competing for a few places. If the hold-up is caused by workmen carrying out repairs it may of course be simply an image taken from experience in life, especially if this is a regular source of irritation and inconvenience. However, such images can also have a symbolic significance which is to reflect our suspicion that our own ambition and efforts are being undermined by other people who are creating unnecessary difficulties or impeding our progress.

To dream of breaking down on a motorway can indicate either a fear of having a mental, physical or emotional crisis caused by severe stress, or a realization that a period of rest and reassessment of our priorities is necessary.

Dreaming of trying to get onto a motorway (usually in an unsuitable vehicle such as a bicycle or on foot) while the traffic roars past at great speed expresses a fear of not being able to get back into work after a period of inactivity and of feeling anxious about being fit enough for a competitive and demanding situation, whether it is work, study or domestic.

## TYPES OF LOCOMOTION

Walking implies a leisurely attitude to life, but can also indicate a need to be alone, to be independent and to be able to follow one's own instinct rather than be 'driven' or led by others. It is not uncommon for someone who is restless in spirit to dream of renouncing the world and walking off into unknown sections of a city or making a pilgrimage into a foreign land. In either case it could be revealing to recall and analyze the character of anyone we meet to find out if we are in search of a neglected aspect of ourselves or a quality that we associate with and admire in someone else.

The character of the scenery that we walk through and the features that we find there will give further clues as to what we are seeking to find or even possibly what we wish to leave behind. Dreaming that we are riding a bicycle or a horse suggests both a wish to have the time to enjoy what we value most, but also a need to control our own emotions and the actions of others. However, bicycles have a secondary significance originating in the memorable moment when we first learn to ride a bike and have our first taste of independence from the parent. That sense of new possibilities can be recalled in a dream to mirror a similar sensation when we overcome a difficulty or achieve greater independence in our adult waking life.

## CARRIAGES

Driving a horse-drawn carriage, cart or Romany caravan implies a restless nature and a conflict between an urge to break free of present commitments and an awareness of our everyday responsibilities.

## MOTORBIKES

Riding a motorbike suggests a certain frustration with the present situation and the need to find a release or channel for that anger and excess energy. Motorbikes have a similar symbolic function to that of horses, although there is an added element of danger due to the speed, which could be implying that the dreamer has a need to take calculated risks to keep his or her life interesting. The power and speed associated with a motorbike also implies impatience, strong sexual drive and the urge to dominate somebody or something, perhaps life itself. For older dreamers a motorbike is likely to represent a wish to tap the energies of youth and to sense freedom from responsibilities which they unconsciously consider restricting.

## CARS

In general the act of driving a car represents the urge to make our own way in the world using our own resources and often with an element of impatience. Certain schools of analysis would see a car as a symbol of a woman that the dreamer wishes to possess sexually as reflected in the fact that most men speak of their car in feminine terms, but in most dreams cars serve as a wish for greater social status and respect. They can also be seen as vehicles of our own dream ego, as an extension of our driving passions, physique, preoccupations and emotions.

A study of the car's condition and performance will tell us a lot about our attitudes to these. For example, any concerns about the body work, reflected in rust or dulling paint work and chrome, could be an indication of concerns about ageing and getting out of condition. Dreams of tinkering with the engine would be reflecting unconscious concerns about the heart, while problems with the electronics would be warning against stress and overwork.

Driving a car in a dream reflects the need to be in control, although the type and condition of the car might be the more significant factor and quite revealing. A sleek, flashy model which is crammed with parking tickets, cigarette butts, empty cans of lager and

coverless CDs and cassettes suggests someone who is eager to appear successful, fashionable and fun to be with, but who is really disorganized, casual and overly keen to impress because they do not feel confident enough to rely on their personality.

Being driven by someone else can have a multitude of meanings. We might wish to cruise through life with others making the difficult decisions for us, in which case the dream car is likely to be a luxury model or limousine, or we may like to be surprised by life and not wish to know where we are going.

Alternatively, we may fear that someone else will take control of our life and lead us into unknown territory. Perhaps that other person, symbolized by the driver, is our own Shadow? Or it may be that our own impulses are driving us and that we feel unable to take control and steer ourselves back on the 'straight and narrow'. The image may even be a visual pun signifying a fear of 'being taken for a ride' (that is, being fooled by someone).

Dreaming of trying vainly to overtake another driver implies an obsessive need to 'get ahead' and be recognized as a remarkable individual, particularly in a competitive situation, and despite the fact that someone else may have a clearer view of the road ahead

than the dreamer. However, if the dreamer succeeds in overtaking other drivers and roars ahead of the pack it can be seen as a positive sign that difficulties which had been holding the dreamer back have been overcome, resulting in a new-found confidence and 'inner drive'. Being overtaken by others suggests an intolerance and difficulty in accepting that someone might be better qualified or more suitable in a certain situation than we are.

## PUBLIC TRANSPORT

Buses, being a form of public transport, are usually settings for dreams in which we explore our attitude to society, our instincts to conform and seek safety in numbers as opposed to our impulse to assert our individuality and make our own way in the world. Buses do not have first and second class sections and so they can be used as levelling images, emphasizing our similarity to, or separation from, the rest of society. Perhaps such a dream is encouraging us to consider other people as 'fellow travellers' through life rather than setting them apart from ourselves. Or it could be asking us to consider if we really want to ride along with everyone else simply because it is the easy option.

The English expression 'to miss the bus' means to miss an opportunity. This is the usual meaning of this occurrence in dreams. However, it could be that the dream is suggesting that we might be turning up too late because we do not want to catch the bus, that we do not feel up to competing with the other passengers who are all heading in the same direction.

Trains have a sexual connotation for many analysts who view the train itself as a symbol of masculine virility and the libido, and stations as symbols of a desired female. Such analysts would interpret the following two examples of typical dream imagery involving trains in set ways: a train entering a tunnel would be seen as representing a desire for intercourse, and leaving a train before it arrives at its destination would be read as a fear of premature ejaculation. A more 'innocent' interpretation of trains in dreams contends that they merely reflect our desire to be carried, guided and supported through specific periods of our lives, when we feel that we have put in sufficient effort and the momentum of this effort should carry us at least to the next stage, symbolized by the station. Railway lines are an equally important element of the train theme and appear as symbols of a clearly defined path that we have laid down for ourselves through study or other forms of preparation.

Dreaming of running to catch a train and then missing it is a typical anxiety dream which reflects a fear of not being ready to grasp the opportunities that one has prepared for when they arise. Another is of being on a train without a ticket. This implies that the dreamer feels they do not have the right to take any 'free rides' that life has to offer and that they have to earn their passage through hard work. There is an unconscious fear that they have achieved their professional or social status through false pretences and that one day they will be 'found out', held to account for every piece of good fortune and their comparatively easy life might be taken from them.

## SHIPS

As water is the element symbolic of the emotions and often divides one land mass from another, so dreams featuring ships, rafts and boats invariably symbolize difficult emotional transitions from one significant stage in life to another. The boat represents the physical body within whose protective shell we weather the storms of experience. A small rowing boat or raft would signify that the dreamer feels exposed to the buffeting winds of fate. A fishing boat, cargo vessel or tanker would indicate that life is considered to be all work, offering little opportunity for leisure. A cruise liner would indicate a relaxed attitude to life in general, and possibly a sensual nature. A ferry, with its car decks and association with making short journeys, would suggest that the dreamer is reluctant to let go of worldly 'baggage', possessions, attitudes, beliefs and values at a time when these need to be jettisoned in order for him to make a critical change.

To find the boat in disrepair indicates that we might not be ready to take the trip, no matter how much we might long to reach the far shore. If you discover fellow passengers or a crew aboard who appear willing to pull their weight or join you in the adventure, this implies that all aspects of your personality are prepared for challenges and a change that will benefit the whole person. If you discover that the passengers view you with suspicion or the crew are drunk, mutinous or incompetent, the inference is that there is resistance to change and maturity from the Shadow and less developed aspects of the self.

One of the most positive and revealing images in such dreams is that of the captain, a rare image, but one which, when it appears, proves the presence of a driving, guiding force who has the dreamer's best interests at heart. The captain personifies the Higher Self. His or her appearance will reveal much about the dreamer's true nature.

If the crossing is difficult and the obstacles formidable it indicates that there is inner resistance to change and that a great effort and resolve is needed to overcome this. The meaning of common expressions such as 'it's all plain sailing', 'sailing close to the wind', 'having plans scuppered' and 'sailing stormy waters' will give further clues as to the significance and relevance of the images in waking life.

If we reach land and dock at the harbour, but find the inhabitants hostile or in any way disturbing, the implication is that we may have a tendency to make rash decisions which we later regret, as suggested by the popular expression 'any old port in a storm'.

## AEROPLANES, GLIDERS AND BALLOONS

Dreams of flying by balloon and glider can reflect a longing to be free of terrestrial troubles and instead experience the tranquillity of the celestial realm. More negatively the sense may be taken to mean 'take flight' and flee from obligations. They can also symbolize our lofty ambitions, a desire to soar above the multitude and the mundane or a desire to have a new perspective on a world which we find confusing and intimidating. The distinguishing feature of flight over other forms of transport is that it involves leaving 'Mother Earth'. Dreams of flying or of waiting impatiently for a flight could be seen as a wish to break free of a dominating female figure.

But unless we have a fear of flying, in which case the dream is attempting to help us face the absurdity of our phobia, aircraft imagery is more likely to be reflecting the sensation of being out of the body during the sleep state and not simply a stage in a symbolic journey.

## DIRECTIONS

Becoming lost is a common dream, but if you dream that you have to consult a map or ask for directions it shows that you are resourceful, practical and confident of being able to find your own way out of difficulties. If the signs lead you astray, the people you ask for help speak in a foreign language or the scenery constantly changes in an illogical, surreal fashion, the suggestion is that you feel you are not being understood in waking life and that as soon as you feel you are making progress someone seems to alter the 'rules' or make unreasonable demands on your time and patience. The map symbolizes an awareness of being on a journey and heading for a specific destination, but also of doubts about whether you are taking the best route and whether you are wasting time in unnecessary diversions.

Dreaming that we are on the wrong train, plane or bus and heading in the wrong direction occurs to most of us at least once in our dreaming lives. The situation symbolizes a conflict between where we would like to go in life and where we feel we should go or where we feel life will take us against our will.

## ACCIDENTS AND BREAKDOWNS

Such images imply that the dreamer fears that they have not got what it takes to see their ambitions fulfilled. They can not imagine that they will be 'allowed' a smooth passage through life and so they are anticipating problems to test their reactions and to prepare themselves. Accidents can generally be interpreted as representing the belief that other people will be the source of problems. There is another possibility, though – that we may be creating problems in waking life in order to punish ourselves and so relieve the nagging of our conscience or to delay having to do something that will test our commitment. These 'self-inflicted wounds' are symbolized as accidents in dreams because these are situations where the blame for a misfortune can be attributed to a momentary, and forgivable, lack of concentration.

Burst tyres and mechanical breakdowns symbolize a suspicion that even though we might be fully prepared we may yet be let down by something which is beyond our control. It is common for someone who will shortly be taking an exam or attending a job interview, for example, to dream that their car, train or bike lets them down. This indicates that these dreams are normal anxiety attacks, safety valves to release the emotional pressure we have put ourselves under, brought on by our belief that we have done all that could be expected of us, that we ought to succeed if others can recognize our abilities and that it will not be our fault if we do not pass the exam or are not offered the job.

Dreaming that a vehicle has run out of fuel is stimulated by the same anxieties, but is actually saying that we have exhausted ourselves physically, mentally and emotionally. To dream that you break down and are then the cause of a traffic jam with a lot of irate drivers cursing you as you vainly try to fix your car can symbolize a stage when aggressive impulses which have been suppressed for a long time threaten to become self-destructive. If others are dependent upon you in waking life, such images can represent your unconscious resentment regardless of the fact that you might happily accept the

obligation in waking life. Implicit in the image is also a fear of letting your dependants down or of being forced to let them down through the fault of something beyond your control.

Careering down the road in a vehicle which is out of control is clearly a symbol for the fear of losing control over one's impulses or events in waking life. Even if the dream ends happily, with the vehicle being safely brought to a standstill, it can still have negative implications if the vehicle is steered through crowded city streets as it suggests that the dreamer needs to be seen to be in control and have his or her abilities admired by others.

## TRAFFIC LIGHTS

Being stuck at traffic lights may simply be a warning against being impatient, by forcing us to re-live our frustration and seeing how absurd it looks in the dreamworld, a surreal world where there is no time or purpose. It could also be drawing our attention to the fact that we might be relying on others too much before we act. If we are stuck with the lights at red for a long time, it might be telling us to slow down and take things easier. If the lights stay on yellow, it is probably indicating that we need to spend more time in preparation before presenting our ideas for approval. A green light is encouraging us to go ahead without waiting for a signal from other people who may mean well but whose values and concept of life will be different from our own.

Breaking down, or not being able to start the engine, at a junction while the lights are constantly changing, suggests indecision, specifically an inability to proceed with anything without first getting other people's opinions and then, having done so, not being able to act on them for fear of making the wrong decision.

## DESTINATIONS

Although dreams of travel and transport are frequently more concerned with the journey than the destination, if we do catch sight of our objective we should be able to understand our present situation more fully. While we are working towards qualifications or climbing the career ladder, we may dream of our ultimate destination as an incentive to make greater effort or to remind us what we are working for when we despair at achieving it.

However, catching a glimpse of our goal is not always an incentive to double our efforts as it is not always what we think we are working towards! The dream might reveal that there is a conflict between what our ego wants to achieve and what our 'better nature' is trying to steer us towards. For example, we might have an exceptional talent for sport or the arts and regularly dream of travelling to a stadium or concert hall, but if we arrive to find ourselves in the stand or the stalls it could be a hint that we are struggling against the odds to be a star player or performer and that our destiny really lies in teaching, coaching or being a commentator or critic. Conversely, if we dream of reaching a particularly exotic, grandiose or idyllic location, it could be to test our reaction and encourage us to question whether this is what we really want for ourselves.

If the destination is merely the terminus, airport or railway station at the end of the line, as it would be in real life, then the dream is indicating a desire for the resolution of a persistent problem or simply the need for rest. It can also be reflecting the fact that the goal which we are working towards has to be approached in a logical step-by-step sequence and that if we do so we will reach a logical and satisfactory conclusion.

# The World Within

IT IS SAID THAT we choose our homes, furnishings and possessions to give expression to the world within: our personality, our habits and our attitudes. In this scheme of things, buildings assume a significance that we might not be consciously aware of – hospitals can reveal facts and fears about our health, libraries and museums can give access to memories, while airports, railway stations and coach terminals can tell us much about our passage through life.

Dreaming of a familiar landscape or the house in which we once lived is likely to be a straightforward recollection or wish-fulfilment. Buildings or landscapes which are not immediately recognizable may have greater significance as they frequently symbolize us or someone we know. The condition of a building, its various rooms and the surrounding terrain can reveal a lot about the state of the dreamer's mind, attitude to the outside world, emotions and health.

There is also a metaphysical dimension to the dream landscape, the key to which is encoded in the biblical phrase "In my Father's house there are many mansions". This is said to refer to the numerous planes of existence in the heavenly realms which we can occasionally visit in our sleep and in which we are said to receive guidance and instruction to help us in our waking lives. So, if you wake with a vague recollection of having been told something of great importance in your sleep, do not dismiss it out of hand as pure fantasy.

## BUILDINGS

Buildings in the dreamscape, particularly houses, invariably represent ourselves, either as we are in life, as we imagine others see us or as we see ourselves. A formidable fortress, for example, suggests a defensive, insular and wary individual; a castle could imply a chilly, secretive personality or a romantic self-contained idealist depending on the style and furnishings. A small cottage could indicate a fussy, old-fashioned stay-at-home type who has little time for outsiders and tries to cram too much into life or, alternatively, a neat, outwardly quiet but inwardly industrious individual entirely dependent on his own resources.

While it might be expected that mansions are symbolic of ambition or success, it is more likely that this image appears as a warning against taking on too many commitments. If the atmosphere of a large house is unsettling, it could be that it indicates the existence of repressed memories as symbolized by the dozens of unexplored rooms.

However, appearances may be deceptive. As with people, the exterior of symbolic buildings may be in stark contrast to the interior, indicating that the dreamer is putting on a 'front' or façade. As we all do this unconsciously to one degree or another, it can be very revealing to examine these dreams in detail.

Attention should also be paid to the condition of the building. A scruffy exterior suggests someone who does not value his appearance, while an overly decorative façade might hide an empty interior.

## PLACES OF WORSHIP

Churches, temples, mosques and other places of worship are often interpreted as religious symbols. However, they are more likely to represent actual places of introspection and reflection within the individual, an inner sanctuary within the psyche free from associations with any specific tradition or belief. As such, these images can indicate a real experience, the moment when the veil between the conscious and the unconscious mind is temporarily drawn aside and we make a connection with our Higher Self. If the dreamer is not bound by religious conditioning the scene might instead be a beautiful garden, a deserted beach or any place of natural beauty and serenity.

Such a dream does not necessarily have spiritual significance. The quality of the experience will indicate whether you have had a 'regular' dream or achieved a higher state of consciousness. With the latter there will be a sensation of having entered a 'sacred space' and a strong 'afterglow' will persist after waking. Such 'dreams' can convey a specific

message verbally or through a symbolic image. Often, however, their purpose is simply to reassure us that we are not alone in waking life.

## MUSEUMS

Museum artefacts and exhibits can symbolize memories and a preoccupation with the past, but more often they preserve the Shadow in all its disguises. The unconscious might use the symbol of a museum exhibit because otherwise we might not wish to face or reflect on these neglected aspects of our personality. Rarely do we acknowledge the Shadow for what it is when it appears in our dreams. If it appears to us in the forms of statues or life-like mannequins we are not too self-conscious to stare and ponder its significance. Statues and mannequins might also appear as impressions from our past lives or as symbols of our frustrated ambitions. If you suspect this, consider their attitude, costumes and accoutrements for clues as to what exactly has been 'frozen' in this form and what relevance it might have to your situation.

## SCHOOLS, COLLEGES AND UNIVERSITIES

Our attitudes towards society and the state are largely the result of our experience of school, which, as a closed community with its own rules and values, can be seen as offering a rehearsal for later life. The intensity and sensitivity of childhood and adolescent emotions is often used by the unconscious to focus us on the causes and consequences of conflict in adulthood. However, when interpreting dreams with a school setting, it should be remembered that the school's values may have coloured our own. Such dreams may be trying to resolve a conflict between the standards of achievement demanded by the school and our expectations of ourselves.

To dream of being back at school long after you have left is a very common theme. You may be uncertain of which way to proceed at present and have returned to schooldays to reassess the future from that perspective. Or, you may be afraid that someone in authority (symbolized by the school), possibly a parent, may wipe out the progress you have made in adult life and return you to a position of dependence.

If the dream is set in a college or university the implication is that there were lessons to be learnt from past experiences which are relevant to the present situation and that they should be considered carefully before you commit yourself to a particular course of action.

## HOSPITALS

Hospitals are synonymous with health and with cleanliness. To dream of being in a hospital as a patient or visitor is likely to indicate that you are concerned about your health or that of someone else. However, it could also suggest that you need to take time out to rest and recuperate from other pressures of waking life. Wandering through an empty hospital looking for the exit suggests that your present situation is in danger of becoming sterile.

## AIRPORTS, RAILWAY STATIONS AND COACH TERMINALS

All of these buildings are symbolic of stages in life's journey. To find oneself at an airport indicates the end of significant changes for the present or that significant changes are ahead. The context and other details should give a clue as to which is the case.

Railway stations are suggestive of a logical progression from one station in life to another at a pace which allows the dreamer to consider each in turn and reflect on the consequences. Coach terminals are more likely to symbolize leaving the past behind and starting out anew.

## TOWERS

A common phallic symbol but one which may have a significance other than sexual. If the tower is well-built and appears impregnable, it could represent a male figure you admire, such as your father or a teacher, or an authority figure you despair of getting through to. A crumbling tower might represent a male whom you see as fallible or flawed in some way.

## LIBRARIES

In the real world we associate libraries primarily with knowledge. In the dreamworld of the unconscious they symbolize memories. To search for a book is to search for a specific memory or detail. To stagger under a pile of heavy books or see yourself furiously leafing through books while the staff are waiting to close for the night signifies being burdened with a memory that has been repressed.

If you are repeatedly plagued by such dreams and awake from them anxious and troubled, try re-entering the dream and calmly imagine yourself asking the librarian to help you search. The library staff may be mere authority figures, but if the dream is an intensely emotional one, they are more likely to be aspects of your personality, probably the part that holds the repressed memory. If this is the case, they can be encouraged to give up their secret. If you suspect the memory is painful or traumatic, you should seek professional help to uncover it.

## BANKS

Banks and building societies often enter our dreams transformed from custodians of our money to symbols of authority whom we feel we must appease. No matter how much money we might have in reality the banks in our dreams will assume a form that is certain to undermine our emotional stability, security and self-assurance. Whenever we become too complacent, particularly with regard to having our emotions under control, the unconscious will use our ambiguous attitude to officialdom in general and such institutions in particular to force us to face the unpalatable fact that we can be easily destabilized if faced with irrational demands, unreasonable expectations or false accusations.

It is common for a financially secure person to dream that his bank manager has called him in to demand the repayment of a loan or overdraft that he does not have in waking life, or to dream that his property and possessions are being repossessed without any reason being given.

The positive aspect of such disturbing dreams is that they often become so surreal and incredible that we soon realize we are only dreaming and can then trigger a lucid dream to resolve our sense of insecurity (see Lucid Dreaming, pages 28–29).

## SHOPS

Shops symbolize a choice that needs to be made. They can also represent a tendency to be frivolous and may even contain a warning to be more careful about money, or, conversely, to be more generous and carefree. Whatever is seen in a shop window could be considered as being either desirable or superficial, as expressed in the phrase, 'it's mere window dressing', depending on your reaction.

If you dream of seeing a person you know either working in a shop, dressing a shop window or sitting in the window as themselves or a life-like mannequin it could be that you have a secret passion for them, or that you consider them to be a mere 'dummy'! If you find yourself sitting in a shop window while passersby stare and comment on the way you look and you feel uncomfortable, it implies that you are concerned about your appearance. If, however, you care little about their reaction it suggests that you probably distrust other people to be open about their true feelings and that you might suspect that they are talking about you behind your back.

## CIRCUSES, CARNIVALS AND FUNFAIRS

Such settings could be encouraging the dreamer to be less intense and return to the carefree attitude of childhood, a message emphasized by the gaudy, primary colours; toys in a dream may be conveying a similar message. However, there is also a certain melancholic quality associated with such places, where the clowns might be seen to bear fixed smiles, where wild animals perform tricks for our amusement and the rootless lifestyle of stall holders and performers symbolizes the outsider. No matter how subtle these impressions might be, they have a resonance which the unconscious mind can use in order to force us to face certain facts or feelings.

One of the most common dreams with a circus setting is that in which we are pulled from the audience to take over from a juggler and find ourselves in the spotlight, paralyzed with fear. A variation would have the dreamer tossing the balls, hoops or skittles only to fumble and drop them to the jeers of the crowd. Such scenarios are typical for people who fear they have taken on too many commitments.

To dream of being in the ring, or a cage, with wild animals, or of putting one's head in a lion's mouth reflects a fear of putting oneself in unnecessary danger, a not uncommon dream for someone who feels himself pressured into accepting a job for which he feels unqualified, or is in a relationship which he unconsciously suspects will savage him emotionally.

To watch wild animals performing tricks symbolizes the guilt of having stripped others of their dignity, perhaps by putting them down in front of colleagues or friends. If we see ourselves performing tricks at the whim of a sadistic ringmaster the dream may be reflecting a belief that we are being forced to live according to the dictates and expectations of others. The ringmaster might indeed actually have the features of the particular individual who we feel is literally 'putting us through the hoop'.

To watch the clowns with a feeling of sadness indicates that we feel life is a sham and that other people are not to be trusted to show their true feelings. There may even be an underlying worry that at present we cannot subscribe to the possibility of lasting happiness.

Enjoyment of the rides at a carnival or funfair suggests the repression of a sensualist nature. A terrifying ride would indicate a fear of losing control of events.

## DOORS AND WINDOWS

Doors generally symbolize new opportunities and an individual's openness to the outside world and the influence of others. The door will be appropriate to the building – one would expect an old-fashioned door fronting a cottage, for example – and it will contain enough variations to give clues to your present emotional and mental state. If, for example, this old-fashioned door is heavy and stiff it suggests that you consider life to be particularly difficult at the moment. An imposing door indicates that you may be anxious about changes to come or new opportunities that you are considering.

If one door opens upon another and yet another beyond that, the implication is that you fear that you will never get the answers that you seek or you are concerned that life is leading you nowhere in particular.

The house symbolizes the psyche and an open door can be seen as indicating a willingness to explore previously neglected aspects of the personality. To face a closed door can mean a fear of self-analysis, a fear of being excluded from society or of being rejected out of hand without having a chance to voice your opinion. The type of building should give a clue as to which of these situations the dream is referring. It may be that you wish to exclude yourself or are regretting being open with other people. The colour of the door should also be considered, as this could hold more vital clues. A locked door indicates frustration at being excluded from work or social activities or of not being able to 'get through' to someone to make them aware of your point of view.

If something has been left outside the door by someone else it suggests that you suspect them of making trouble behind your back, as expressed in the phrase 'to lay the blame at someone else's door'. If it is you who left something by someone else's door, this suggests that you feel guilty for having accused them of something.

Windows are associated with sight, though usually in the sense of inner visions, sometimes even of the future. Whatever you see through the window represents your view of the world. The style of the window symbolizes the breadth of your vision, or the depth of your insight. If the view is expansive and attractive it indicates optimism. If the window is narrow or the view is obscured by a high wall or ugly, imposing buildings, this suggests that you are imposing limitations and unreasonably high expectations on yourself which you know cannot be met. Such dreams indicate a fear of success and tend to occur when we have conflicting emotions concerning a particular ambition. Small windows suggest the need for privacy and possibly even a distrust of outsiders, while large picture windows represent flamboyance and openness.

Windows let light in. Light flooding into a room in the dream world is symbolic of insight. If the curtains are drawn the implication is that we wish to block ourselves off from certain facts or outside influences. Drawing the curtains back indicates a willingness to face the facts.

## GATES

Gates traditionally represent a relationship with a partner. Heavy, ornate gates suggest a

partner who is considered to be putting up some form of resistance, perhaps to a change of job or a move to another home. It might even be the refusal to acknowledge the dreamer's need for space in which to grow emotionally, although expressed through a subtle resistance to change of which only the unconscious is aware. Rusty old-fashioned gates can narrow the problem down to the partner's stubborn insistence of leaving the situation as it is despite signs that change will be good for both parties. A small gate implies a partner who is considered too compliant. A gate swinging on a broken hinge suggests that the couple are going through a difficult period, but that the dreamer believes it is possible to repair the relationship.

## INTERIORS

Entering our own house in a dream indicates a need to explore our inner selves. If the dream continues beyond this point it could prove very revealing as to what aspects of our selves are being undervalued or neglected.

In the dreamhouse each room has a symbolic significance, either physical or psychological. This means that a dream focusing on a particular room has two possible interpretations (see also Jung and the House of the Psyche, pages 14–15 and Dreamhouse of the Psyche exercise on pages 24–25). In general the ground floor is symbolic of the unconscious mind, with the upper rooms representing the conscious mind. The attic symbolizes the intellect, ideas and memories, and the basement the instincts.

## CORRIDORS, PASSAGES AND HALLWAYS

These are often seen as being symbolic of a transition from one stage of life to another. To Freudian analysts a dream featuring a corridor, hallway or passage (according to Freud, all symbols of the vagina) with no obvious exit would indicate a wish to have sexual intercourse with whomever the house represents. If these linking images are narrow and ill-lit, one interpretation might be that the dreamer feels restricted in his waking life and has no clear idea of his purpose or direction.

## ATTIC

A cramped and crowded attic indicates confusion and an unwillingness to let go of the past. An airy, orderly and well illuminated attic indicates clarity of thought and a healthy attitude to the past. On a physical level the attic corresponds to the head, although in the unconscious this may symbolize the entire house. (Following this latter symbolic track the door would then correspond to the mouth and the eyes to the windows. Dirty or cracked windows would imply blindness to certain facts the dreamer does not want to acknowledge. An open door might indicate a tendency to speak before thinking matters through properly. A closed door would indicate a reluctance to voice an opinion, perhaps because the dreamer believes he is always criticized when he does so. Closed shutters or boarded up doors and windows might provide confirmation of this.)

## BEDROOM

Bedrooms are places of rest as well as of sexual pleasure. We may dream of retreating to a luxurious bedroom to reflect our unconscious need to escape the stress and strain of waking life. Although we might be unaware of it, there is a constant struggle between the conscious mind which seeks continual stimulus and the unconscious which seeks stillness. Dreaming of bedrooms and other symbols of rest, such as desert islands, deserted beaches and secluded gardens, is the unconscious mind's most effective method of prompting us to reconsider our priorities.

Bedrooms also double as dressing rooms, where we put on the costumes we need to act our part in the world. A bedroom setting can reveal a lot about who we think we are and who we think we ought to be. Time spent looking in the mirror in a dream is not necessarily indicative of a narcissistic nature, and might imply a curiosity about our true identity. If we conspicuously avoid looking in the mirror, or there is no mirror in the bedroom (a revealing detail in itself), it suggests the need to avoid facing a fact that we believe is obvious to everyone else.

## LOUNGE

The lounge or living room is the space in which we unwind, watch television, listen to music, read and perhaps entertain friends or family. But do we really relax here or simply pass the time? A dream centring on this room may reveal the truth. If your lounge is the centre of family life, a dream focused on this room may reveal family tensions.

On both a physical and emotional level the lounge corresponds to the heart. Dreams of happy family gatherings or snuggling close to a loved one on the sofa indicate a warm, considerate nature. An empty living room or one where the inhabitants are squabbling or sitting apart suggests a reluctance to share emotions.

## KITCHEN OR DINING ROOM

Food is symbolic of emotional and spiritual nourishment and so the state of the kitchen and the atmosphere in the dining room can reveal our attitude to family and friends.

If the dreamer lives alone and in the dream both rooms are spotless and tidy (regardless of how these rooms look in waking life), this could reflect the fact that he or she is not prepared to risk sharing emotions or making commitments to others. If the dreamer lives alone and both rooms are a complete mess (again, regardless of the fact that in real life these rooms might be tidy), this suggests a tendency to being self-centred, thick-skinned and oblivious to criticism.

If the dreamer has a family and these rooms are relatively clean and tidy, this indicates that there is enough space for self-expression. However, if the rooms are eerily quiet and deserted it could suggest a feeling that the family is not close enough or comfortable with sharing emotions. If there are signs that the rooms are being actively used, it indicates that the family members are, in a sense, nourishing one another. But if the dining table is littered with half-eaten meals and the kitchen sink is crowded with dirty dishes, it suggests a fear that the family is refusing to air its problems and is losing its ability to communicate.

A well-stocked kitchen symbolizes that the dreamer is mentally prepared for unexpected events and is unlikely to be unsettled or distracted by unpredictable problems.

## BATHROOM AND TOILET

These two rooms have an association with cleanliness, privacy and plumbing which the unconscious mind draws upon to raise issues of health (particularly stomach complaints) and feelings of vulnerability.

## CELLAR OR BASEMENT

Rooms below ground level symbolize repressed impulses, primitive instincts and our deepest fears. That is one reason why we all share a fear of what might lie hidden in the shadows of a cellar. Basements also have a physical association with the stomach and bowels. So, if there is a boiler which has broken down or is straining to capacity, it could be that the dream is warning against over-indulging in food to compensate for a lack of affection or interest in life.

## STAIRS

Stairs link levels of consciousness and are generally symbolic of progress or the desire to make progress. The question you need to consider is whether the stairs in your dream were narrow or wide, winding or straight, steep, grand and imposing or merely austere and functional.

In the dreamscape the ideal stairs are wide and easy to climb or descend. If you find yourself stuck halfway with no sense of whether to go up or down, this suggests indecision, fear of commitment and lack of progress. Descending a flight of stairs to the ground floor should not be seen as negative, but simply as a return

to a normal state of awareness. A descent to the basement can be significant as invariably it symbolizes either the subconscious or the bowels, depending on the context of the dream and what is discovered there (see Cellar or Basement, page 108).

Being a part of the structure of a building, stairs are frequently representative of a dreamer's attitude to home life. Narrow stairs imply restriction, while grand staircases symbolize flamboyance and freedom to express emotions at home. A staircase with bare boards indicates either that something within the family unit is unresolved or something in the house itself remains unfinished. A functionally carpeted staircase might imply a current situation or relationship which is regarded by the dreamer as either temporary or lacking any emotional depth. A plush, luxuriously carpeted staircase suggests the dreamer has a feeling of security and contentment at home.

## PAINTINGS, PICTURES AND ORNAMENTS

The presence in a dream of paintings, pictures and photographs suggests that people are important to the dreamer. Ornaments speak of significant memories. As the building itself invariably symbolizes the dreamer, portraits or photographs often reveal the dreamer's 'true' character.

## FURNITURE

The style of furniture will reveal whether the dreamer is habitually looking to the past or giving full attention to the present. If the furniture is antique but well cared for the implication is that memories are cherished. If it is shrouded in dustsheets, it could indicate that the dreamer is not prepared to face certain episodes in the past. A house crammed with ugly or functional furniture indicates a fear of restriction. Furniture that is attractive to the dreamer suggests difficulty in restraining impulses, delegating responsibility or saying 'No' when pressured by other people.

Small chairs hint at low self-esteem, while large chairs boast of confidence. Soft, comfortable chairs imply a tendency to take things easy and perhaps not to throw oneself fully into work or family activities. Hard chairs suggest restlessness, difficulties at work or school and possibly a need to make changes or move on. A single empty chair in a prominent position might imply that the dreamer feels under intense scrutiny at the present time, and is anxious about being put 'under the spotlight' for further 'interrogation'. This image can also symbolize loss, either of a person to whom the dreamer wishes to speak, or of something fondly remembered from the past, possibly even an aspect of the Self which it is feared can not be revitalized.

The presence of desks, chests of drawers and cabinets indicates a well-organized and orderly temperament. It may also hint at something which has been put away because it cannot be faced. Freudians see chests of drawers as symbolizing women and if the drawers hold sexy lingerie, it implies a reluctance to accept one's sexuality. A cabinet which is thought to contain toys suggests anxiety concerning childhood memories. If the cabinet contains photographs, attention is being drawn to the dreamer's relationship to the people in the photographs. The desire to open a locked chest, desk or cabinet but not be able to find the key is symbolic of the dreamer's conflicting emotions concerning the memories and emotions which the artefacts represent.

Book cases are associated with learning although in certain contexts they can assume greater significance. A fairly common theme is to dream of searching the shelves and among the books on them for something of great importance which can not be recalled. This is symbolic of the dream ego's search through the unconscious for a vital piece of information that could hold the key to an irrational impulse, phobia or fear, or even a repressed memory which has significance for the dreamer's present situation.

Wardrobes in dreams disguise or emphasize our true identities, and, by inference, our feelings. When we feel depressed we can 'dress up' or lose ourselves in a uniform, formal wear, casual wear or fancy dress. This may be reflected by the prominence of a wardrobe in a dream. Wardrobes were also once a favourite hiding place for children during play. Many an adult nightmare concerning fear of being locked in a wardrobe or cupboard has its origins in such a game.

In dreams tables serve the same function as an altar. They are a focus for sacrifice or worship. Whatever objects are found upon it are either to be given up for the highest good of the dreamer or set aside for special attention because they have been undervalued in waking life.

## PACKING CASES

Unopened packing cases suggest a lack of commitment, an unsettled disposition and a fear of responsibility. If you suspect or discover that the cases contain significant objects the implication is that you have put whatever these symbolize to the back of your mind and that it is now time to reconsider their relevance to your present situation. If you discover that the boxes or cases contain little of value, this indicates that you might be clinging on to outdated attitudes and attachments which could be cluttering up your mind, diverting your attention from what is really

important to you and draining you of vital energy. If the images appear in the context of a move to another, larger house it reflects a desire for more privacy and space to develop free of present restrictions, either within a relationship, the family or at work. If the move involves returning to a previous house where there were problems, it suggests there are deep feelings connected with the period spent in this house and that these have not been accepted or resolved. Such a dream can also reflect a reluctance to accept the present situation as reality and might express the wish to return to a time when there were fewer emotional demands.

## FIREPLACES

Big fireplaces symbolize a passionate nature. Small fireplaces suggest sensitivity and a tendency to keep quiet about feelings. An empty fireplace which is smouldering with the embers of a dying fire implies a fading passion. Finding the charred remains of clothing, letters, diaries or a memento of some sort is an indication of the desire to exorcise the memories or the emotions which these objects represent.

## BEDS

Beds are frequently associated with sexuality, but they can also symbolize the emotional life and temperament of the dreamer. A

hard, lumpy bed represents stress and a difficulty in separating work from private life. A large, soft, decorously draped four-poster bed can be seen as a symbol of a passionate, flamboyant nature, or of the wish to be cosseted from the pressures of waking life. Plain, functional beds suggest a reluctance to trust one's feelings. Waterbeds indicate a fun-loving and possibly frivolous nature.

## CLOCKS

Small, modern functional clocks indicate restlessness or even a nervous nature. A prominent grandfather clock indicates a leisurely, even sedate personality. A clock might also be an obscure reference to the heart, which in colloquial English is still often referred to as 'the old ticker'.

# The World Outside

A CENTRAL CONCEPT of the Western esoteric tradition, which is based on the secret teachings of the Jewish and Christian mystics, states that 'Man contains all that is above in heaven and below upon earth … One man is a world in miniature.' On a purely physical level we can see that our bodies contain the four elements of Fire, Air, Water and Earth in the heat of our skin, the gaseousness of our breath, the liquidity of the blood in our veins and the solidity of the bones which give form to the flesh. We also internalize the physical world at the subtler mental, emotional and spiritual levels, condensing these into symbols which we can analyse to explore our own psyche and our attitudes to the outside world.

Human nature can be as capricious and unpredictable as the forces of the natural world. This affinity with nature is the result of our having evolved through all of the stages of evolution. Consequently, we contain elements of the mineral, vegetable and animal kingdoms imprinted within our psyche and these periodically re-emerge to haunt our dreams.

## GARDENS

Gardens can reveal a lot about the temperament of the dreamer. A tidy, formal garden symbolizes someone organized but perhaps a little rigid and predictable in his habits. A sprawling cottage garden suggests an effusive but casual personality tempted to leave things to take their own course, perhaps because of earlier disappointments.

A vegetable garden or orchard which dominates implies a down-to-earth personality. However, if either is merely a notable feature, it suggests that the dreamer has one eye on the future and is prepared for sudden changes in fortune. A productive plot of home-grown fruit or vegetables can also symbolize the dreamer's desire to 'be fruitful' and raise children. In fact, what is being cultivated can be as significant as the act of cultivation. Citrus fruits, for example, might symbolize a sharp tongue or bitterness towards someone the dreamer holds a grudge against. Herbs represent the wish for a healthier lifestyle. Common vegetables such as carrots, leeks or potatoes symbolize the urge to establish roots and provide the basic necessities of a stable family life.

## GARDENING

A profusion of weeds symbolizes potential problems which are being neglected and allowed to take root in the unconscious. Dreaming of uprooting weeds,

cultivating an overgrown patch of wasteground or landscaping a barren plot of land is symbolic of the dreamer's desire to make a fresh start in life, to take control of destructive habits and for more creative and productive means of self-expression.

If the same ground is being dug over and over again or a series of dreams occurs in which the same patch of ground is dug, this suggests a preoccupation with a problem which we can not accept has been resolved or is now beyond our control. A simple technique for resolving such unsettling dreams can be practised before going to sleep. Imagine that you are standing in the dream garden and writing a note asking for help with the problem. When you have finished the note, see yourself plant it in a hole in the ground. Trust that, just as nature does with weeds, the wish in the note will break down in the soil or be brought to a fruitful conclusion.

If the problem involves a barrier to your ambitions or a residue of feelings which you want to be rid of, imagine it in the form of a thorn bush, large weed or nettle which you dig up and burn, leaving the ashes to be scattered to the winds.

## WALLS AND FENCES

Brick walls indicate formality, self-control and limitations (self-imposed or otherwise). Stone walls suggest a rough charm.

High walls indicate formidable obstacles to be overcome and a desire for privacy or secrecy. Low walls suggest openness, and possibly also lower expectations.

## LANDSCAPES

Landscapes can represent stages in our lives, with what is in the background symbolizing the past, the close terrain symbolizing the present, and whatever lies ahead symbolizing the future as the dreamer imagines it to be.

An unfamiliar landscape relates to our psychological state, in particular to an area of thinking that we have been ignoring or neglecting. A landscape that is strangely familiar can refer to a recurring situation or emotion in waking life which needs to be consciously identified. Through such a dream we are being forced to revisit this place until we recognize it. An idyllic setting is often symbolic of the wish to return to childhood or could be a prompt from the unconscious to take note of childhood qualities, talents, attitudes and ambitions we still possess although we have not fulfilled their potential.

A wide open space can symbolize a sense of or desire for freedom, but also the fear of vulnerability which can result from abandoning a secure and familiar environment. If our current situation is a source of security, it is likely to appear in our dreams as a form of sanctuary, perhaps a park, small garden or secluded woodland. If there is stress or a sense of insecurity at home or work the dream sanctuary may become dark and claustrophobic. Wild, overgrown areas, particularly rainforests and jungles, are common settings for exploring erotic impulses free from the censorship or disapproval of the preconscious mind. Crowded cityscapes are the natural habitat of the ego. Dreams set in a city are likely to express secret or frustrated ambitions and be the setting in which we act out any resentment of other people.

A countryside setting might appear to reflect a state of inner calm and contentment, but this is probably only a reflection of how we like to think of ourselves. Freudians would say that the contours and features of the landscape are symbolic of the human body and the dreamer's wish to have sexual intercourse with whomever the landscape represents, but this only explains a proportion of such dreams. It is worth trying to recall details of the terrain because these should reveal the meaning of the dream.

Mountains suggest high (possibly unrealistic) aspirations and also an expectation of there being difficulties ahead. Gently rolling hills indicate an easy-going nature and woods are symbolic of our attitude to the unknown. Dark woods or forests indicate a fear of what cannot be foreseen. Paths imply that no matter how dark the wood might be, we will find a way through the tough times. Fields are generally the starting point of journeys through the inner landscape and often indicate of our present state of mind. Long grass and weeds imply that something of inner importance has been neglected. Cultivated fields symbolize an orderly, balanced life full of possibilities. Barren fields suggest a temporary loss of vitality and direction. Ploughed fields suggest problems, but can also reflect an unconscious wish to be productive either in work, creativity or raising a family.

Walls can represent emotional barriers as well as expectations. A wall that is straight and secure implies that the emotions are well contained. A crumbling wall suggests an inability to keep our feelings to ourselves. A wall whose stones have collapsed inwards indicates a need to invite others to share our feelings.

Calm water shows that there are no emotional problems at present. Still water might be an encouragement to us to gaze into it and reflect on what we see there whilst deep water suggests that much needs to be explored in the depths of the unconscious. Shallow waters and the proximity of the river bed may be symbolic of a barrier to the unconscious. A fast-flowing stream suggests a healthy emotional balance and our willingness to be carried along by events rather than struggle to 'swim against the tide'. A stream that is running dry or stagnating suggests that we might be experiencing problems in clearing emotional blocks or in finding outlets for self-expression. Clear, sparkling waters, especially in a waterfall, are symbolic of our desire to clear negative emotions and start afresh.

## BRIDGES

Bridges are symbols of transition between the conscious and unconscious and between phases of our lives. The structure of the bridge will indicate whether the crossing will be precarious or easy. A sound structure implies that the passage will be smooth. A rope bridge or a bridge in disrepair indicates difficulties, often of our own making.

## CAVES

For Freudians this image has obvious sexual symbolism. The cave represents a desire to physically and psychologically penetrate the mysteries of the female. At another level the dream can be expressing a wish to return to the safety of the womb, or retreat to a womb-like sanctuary, to recuperate and revitalize ourselves prior to re-emerging in a more highly developed form, as butterflies emerge from their cocoons.

There is also a third level at which this image might have relevance. In dreams, as in many myths and legends, caves often feature as a hiding place for treasure, a universal symbol of the need to explore the deepest recesses of the unconscious in search of the True Self. In these the hero symbolizes the dream ego. The guardian of the cave, traditionally a dragon or dwarf, represents the preconscious 'censor' which prevents us being disturbed by the primal images from the collective unconscious. Slaying the guardian, exploring the cave and returning with the treasure to the surface is symbolic of a process which involves recognizing that our waking consciousness is only a fragment of the True Self. Such dreams are likely to precede an 'awakening' of the individual, who will begin to develop a clearer sense of self with new talents and insights emerging in the subsequent weeks and months.

## GRAVEYARDS, CEMETERIES AND CHURCHYARDS

To dream of wandering among tombstones and mausoleums may seem a morbid pastime, but we all visit such places at least once in our dreams, whenever we are ready to face the fact of our own mortality. We have no conscious memories of the afterlife to call upon and so we use the symbols of death to test our reactions to our own passing and that of others. While wandering among the graves in our dream, we may meet a friend

or loved one who has died and from whom we seek reassurance that something awaits us on 'the other side'. Alternatively, we may say something that we had no opportunity to say to them in life, perhaps to ask forgiveness and unburden ourselves of guilt, or simply to tell them that we still remember them with affection.

There is the possibility that such meetings do actually take place between the deceased and the living in the realm known as the astral plane through which the 'dreambody' can pass during sleep. This would explain the relief, reassurance and sense of peace dreamers experience after such encounters. After all, if these meetings were merely a product of the imagination, would they leave such indelible impressions on dreamers?

On a practical level we talk of things that have been consigned to the past as being 'dead and buried'. It is conceivable that the unconscious might use a cemetery to remind us that something which still troubles us should finally be allowed to 'die'. Or perhaps something which we have 'buried' in our unconscious must de disinterred and dealt with. The fact that the setting is grim may reflect our disgust at having to face the problem.

## TREES

Trees are universal symbols reflecting the phases of human life: the embryo is represented by

the seed, youth envisaged in terms of 'blossoming' and 'branching out' and maturity symbolized in the production of fruit or new seed (that is a family of our own). Many cultures, philosophies and religious traditions have adopted the tree as a symbol of the belief that human beings are the connecting point of celestial and terrestrial forces: man is envisaged as the trunk of the tree with branches stretching to the heavens and roots penetrating the ground.

A single tree featuring prominently in a dream is therefore likely to symbolize the individual, his or her family (as reflected in the expression 'a family tree') or the human 'family' and its various 'branches'. A single oak, or any tree associated with strength or having a phallic shape, will represent a specific male. A fragrant flowering fruit or ornamental tree can be symbolic of a specific female. If the tree is ancient and awe-inspiring it could be a sign of the symbolic awakening of the dreamer's Higher Self and sense of union with the universal creative force.

On another level, wandering among trees in a forest can represent a curiosity about the nature of the unconscious. Wood is another symbol of the unconscious, it being derived from a living, growing source which remains impenetrable to the conscious mind.

## PLANTS AND FLOWERS

Flowers are universal symbols of beauty, gentleness, innocence, purity and perfection. Faded and crushed flowers often appear in dreams, as they do in movies, to represent defloration, rape or innocence defiled. Dried flowers imply a loss of vitality.

It used to be fashionable to name children after plants in the belief that plants symbolized specific qualities or characteristics. Roses, for example, were deemed to be beautiful and violets modest, as in the phrase 'she is a shrinking violet'. For this reason dreaming of specific plants and flowers which have been used in this way can be a reference to a particular person of the same name. However, it is also worth considering the traditional associations or uses of that plant.

### IRIS

With its sword-shaped leaves and association with the Virgin Mary the Iris has become a Christian symbol of suffering.

### LILY

In the Christian tradition the lily is a symbol of purity and piety. This view derives from a reference to it in the Sermon on the Mount in which Jesus compared all those who renounced wealth to this elegant, pure, white flower. However, in pagan tradition the lily has erotic connotations due to its heady fragrance and phallic-shaped pistil.

### LOTUS

The lotus has long been a symbol of immortality, perfection and rebirth, dating back to ancient Egypt where its rise from the mud was considered a metaphor for the act of creation. Today it is more commonly associated with the gradual process of spiritual awakening, as represented in the image of the gently unfolding white lotus adopted by Buddhists and other eastern philosophies.

### VIOLET

With their mingling of red and blue, colours associated with physical action and celestial tranquillity, violets indicate a transitional period from intense activity to that of calm reflection.

### PANSIES

Pansies are symbols of fond remembrance, an association derived from their heart-like shape. If you find yourself picking them in a dream it may be a reminder to keep in touch with someone you have neglected. Perhaps the flowers symbolize the memory of someone whose death you are still finding it difficult to acknowledge?

### CARNATION

Pink carnations appear in several major paintings of the Madonna and child as symbols of selfless maternal love. Recently the use of pink carnations in bridal bouquets and wedding sprays has made them a modern marriage symbol.

### ROSES

Roses are associated with feminine beauty and fragrance. For centuries the rosebud was a universal symbol of virginity. Red roses are still considered the flowers of romance. However, almost all rose bushes have nasty-looking thorns which might imply that the person or situation they represent in the dream has a deceptively beguiling appearance which hides a sharper side. Standard roses have a proud, formal appearance while climbing and rambling roses have an old-fashioned image associated with cottage gardens. The latter types require support, but otherwise need very little care and bloom profusely for long periods year after year. Could their prominence in a dream set in a cottage garden or old mansion be a reference to an elderly mother or aunt who is fiercely independent but whom you suspect could do with more emotional or financial support?

### POPPY

The black-hearted, blood-red poppy was adopted as a symbol of remembrance after the First World War, and since this time it has been associated with the remembrance of the dead from the two world wars.

Anemones, violets and other red and red-flecked flowers have an association with death that dates back to the blood sacrifices of the Aztecs.

Vines and creepers are symbols of entanglements and tenacious, troublesome individuals who insist on holding us back from carrying out our plans.

## SKY

As with the landscape and environment the appearance of the sky reflects our present view of both the outside world and our inner world. An ominous overcast sky is suggestive of depression and pessimism. A cloudless blue sky indicates optimism and limitless potential.

## SEA

Our fear of and fascination with the sea originates from the earliest stages of our evolution and from the nine months that human embryos spend in the waters of their mother's womb.

The dark, unfathomable depths of the sea are symbolic of the sustaining source of all life, of the unknown and the unpredictable forces of nature. Dreams of waves gently lapping against the shore or lakeside are reminding us that, even if our lives are stormy at present, nothing disturbs the ebb and flow of life, the rhythm of natural forces and the cycle of creation.

## SEASONS

In the dreamworld the backdrop can be as significant as the detail. The traditional interpretation of the seasons as representing the phases of life, with spring

corresponding to childhood, summer to youth, autumn to maturity and winter to old age, are still relevant and revealing. The weather can have great symbolic significance, reflecting the way it dictates our choice of activities and affects our mood.

## SPRING

Spring is the universal symbol of rebirth, vitality and hope. If a dream with a spring setting occurs while you are going through a troubled or unproductive time, it may be reminding you of the momentum for change and growth within each of us which will overcome even the most discouraging conditions. Dreams of spring or those with prominent symbols of the season are prompts from the unconscious to start new ventures, rediscover our youthful enthusiasm or take up physical activities that benefit not only the body but the whole personality.

## SUMMER

Long, hot summer days are synonymous with relaxation, cloudless blue skies, gardens bursting with vibrant colour and the intense heat of the sun. Dreams with a summer setting are symbolic of satisfaction, achievement, revitalizing energies and clear horizons. If the dream does not follow a specific success, such as passing an exam, promotion or being offered a new job, then it is likely to reflect an

inner sense of infinite possibilities and 'plain sailing' ahead. In either case the summer setting might be hinting that now is the ideal time to take a well-deserved holiday.

## AUTUMN

Autumn is traditionally the season of harvesting and of reaping what one has sown. Dreams of autumn are usually rich with vivid fiery colours, particularly orange, which corresponds to the sacral chakra in eastern philosophy, an energy centre in the region of the groin which emphasizes the autumnal theme of procreation and fruition. Images of falling leaves in a dream suggest that it might be prudent to conserve our energy and resources in preparation for the possibility of dark, stormy times ahead.

## WINTER

In general, winter scenes symbolize a withdrawal into the self, as reflected in the animal's instinct to hibernate and man's urge to stay indoors.

The bitterly cold weather and short, dark days associated with the season can symbolize either sexual or psychological frigidity. In the latter case the unconscious could be warning that a vital part of the personality is in danger of being 'frozen out' because it is being denied by the ego. Perhaps it might be suggesting that something in danger of becoming an obsession should be 'frozen' for the time being because it cannot be fully understood in our present state of mind. In this case winter imagery is being used to emphasize the importance of rest and reflection above action.

To see someone we know isolated in a snow-whitened landscape implies that we consider them to be 'frozen out' of our life and are feeling guilty about it. To see someone we recognize wandering aimlessly through the snow suggests that we consider them to have 'lost their way' metaphorically speaking. To see that same person struggling through the snow is a reflection of our sympathy for them. A trail of footprints left in the snow signifies our secret admiration for that person and our desire to follow him or her. However, if we come upon a trail of footprints in the course of the dream and the person who made them is not in sight, this symbolizes a suspicion that we have not been fully taken into the confidence of someone to whom we are close.

Images of bleakness and cold are invariably symbolic of suffering. However, these same images of frozen ground could be telling us that the present is not the right time to sow the seeds of future projects or to try and 'break new ground'. The virgin white snow of winter forming a purifying blanket over the dream scenery can signify a need to wipe the mind clean of something which threatens to disturb our peace. Alternatively, the snow may appear in our dreams in order to bury something we wish to forget.

Winter images of frozen lakes may illustrate that we are 'skating on thin ice', indicating that our situation might be difficult and potentially dangerous. It could imply that we are not getting a firm grip on things and we fear the possibility of slipping up.

Winter scenes can provide positive messages too, reminding us of a happy childhood when the season held the promise of skating, sledging, building a snowman and, of course, Christmas festivities. Such dreams would be encouraging us not to take life too seriously but to rekindle some of the wonder and enthusiasm of childhood.

## WEATHER

Storms are symbolic of strong pent-up emotions and can indicate intense mental stress. Such images signify the need to release frustrations and 'ground' repressed anger, just as lightning dissipates the build-up of energy in the atmosphere during a thunderstorm. Ominous thunder clouds can represent a sense of impending disaster, whether there is any real basis for that belief or not. Lightning is a more positive image, although it might be disturbing in the dream itself. Flashes of lightning symbolize illumination and intuition. The question to ask is what was being illuminated. In dreams of this type the landscape is most likely to represent our past, present and future (see page 114) with the storm gathering either behind or in front of us. The flashes of lightning will reveal the source of fears or problems originating in the past, or the likely consequences of actions taken in the present. People and scenes, real or imagined, might also be momentarily lit by the lightning, giving snapshot-like images of repressed memories which are struggling to get through to the conscious mind. Other flashes might simply reveal what the dreamer unconsciously thinks of that person!

## STORMS

Violent, destructive storms often indicate something that needs to be cleared – an unconscious reference perhaps to the expression 'the wind of change'. The storm may also be a substitute image for something we fear. In this case the storm image is being used because it is something of which it is socially acceptable to be frightened whereas what we really fear might be our own uncontrollable instincts or impulses.

If the dreamer is carried along by a strong wind the inference is of conflict between an awareness of a need to move on (to a new home or job perhaps) and a reluctance to leave what is secure and familiar.

## MIST OR FOG

Mist or fog indicates that something is being hidden from the conscious mind or obscured by a 'smokescreen' of incidental or misleading information. Again, it could be something which symbolizes a repressed memory, possibly of a traumatic car accident for which fog or mist would be an appropriate 'screen'. A dream with either of these weather features might also indicate a temporary loss of direction in waking life.

## RAIN

Although rain is traditionally seen as symbolizing tears and therefore sadness, its appearance in a dream suggests that the present is a period of revitalization and cleansing. In the physical realm rain clears the air, refreshes plant life and makes arid ground fertile and productive, thus it is an ideal symbol by which the unconscious conveys a similar message. The one negative image sees the dreamer forced to remain inside because of a downpour, symbolizing the tendency to have one's enthusiasm dampened or to put off what needs to be done whilst blaming it on external factors.

## SUNSHINE

Sunshine is a strong, positive symbol of contentment and well-being. Yellow, the colour we associate with the sun, is symbolic of healing and the emotions, so dreams of the sun breaking through dark clouds suggest that a difficult time has passed and that now is a time for relaxation. To see a landscape or city streets gilded by sunlight indicates that plans have been well thought through and that the way ahead appears clear of obvious problems.

## THE ELEMENTS

The four elements of fire, water, earth and air are considered to be both the primary constituents of the cosmos and of all life within it. As human beings are a microcosm, a universe in miniature, the same four elements can be seen as corresponding to our passions, characteristics, qualities and attributes. Traditionally, water and earth are seen as symbolic of the passive, feminine principle, while fire and air represent the active, masculine principle.

## EARTH

We talk of people as being 'down to earth', or of their need to 'come down to earth', as reflecting a need to be 'rooted' and 'grounded' in the 'real' world. Earth symbolizes a practical nature and the quality of common sense, someone who is hard working, conscious of the matter in hand and not given to daydreams, unrealistic ambitions or irrational impulses. It is a key symbol of stability.

Dreaming of ploughing, gardening, digging the foundations for a house or simply walking in the countryside are all expressions of the need to cultivate and appreciate these qualities as essential for maintaining an emotional balance in the material world.

The negative aspect of earth can be symbolized by dreams of being stuck in mud. These warn against the danger of becoming bogged down with detail or weighed down with responsibility. Dreams of digging oneself into a hole suggest a stubborn nature and the tendency to create obstacles for oneself, a characteristic enforced by the term 'earthy', which implies a person who is rough in manner and lacking imagination.

Countryside images, particularly those illustrating cultivation of the land, may be referring to 'Mother Earth', or to the passive feminine principle and the creative, nurturing aspect of human nature.

## AIR

Air is symbolic of the divine, animating spirit, the soul, which is equated with the breath in man and the wind in nature. Because it is the one invisible element, it is usually symbolized in dreams as a breeze which might carry the dreamer up to the clouds in a balloon, emphasizing the divine origin and freedom of the human spirit or simply the dreamer's buoyant mood. However, if we have neglected the development of the inner self, we might dream of a strong wind rattling the windows of our house to remind us of the impermanence of things we value in the material world. Air can also be a cooling agent and might feature in dreams – perhaps of sailing on a summer's day – which could be interpreted as telling us to cool down and take things a little easier.

In many myths and legends the gods and departed spirits sent their messages to the living in the form of winds. This symbolism can occur in our dreams where telepathic communication with someone we have been close to might be received in the form of such imagery. Perhaps we might dream of being in their house as it once was with a breeze ruffling the curtains to draw our attention to a picture of the person who wishes to be remembered.

The allusion to communication might be carried through on a more mundane level where someone who is all bluster and little substance might be depicted in some way so as to emphasize the fact that we think of them as being 'full of hot air'.

## WATER

Water symbolizes the fluidity of the emotions and the depths of the unconscious. Calm, clear waters suggest serenity, contentment and insight. Murky, turbulent waters symbolize clouded judgement and emotional disturbance, the one usually affecting the other. Deep waters can represent either a depth of feeling for someone or something or be hinting that we must be prepared to plunge into the unknown to find what we are looking for. Shallow water indicates less intense emotions and implies that what is sought will be found near the surface – an obvious fact known to the conscious mind but one which, for some reason, is not being acknowledged. Fast-flowing water can represent channelled energy which is seeking release, perhaps in physical activity, as the unconscious will be making a connection with historical and modern water-powered wheels and engines.

Water is an emotional symbol and the allusion in the dream might be to a form of self-expression, such as music or drama, which will be a more effective means of channelling excess emotional energy. Beware if the dream features a dam – this indicates an unconscious barrier to self-expression, perhaps symbolizing fear of failure, and therefore a conflict between the rational conscious mind and the emotional impulse.

Water is the main theme in a number of typical dreams, of which the following are the most common and significant:

To dream of drowning or being swept away by a flood or the current symbolizes a fear of being out of one's depth, losing control, being swamped by thoughts, impulses and impressions from the unconscious, overwhelmed by a possessive lover or being dragged down by the weight of responsibilities, debts or the demands of other people.

Dreaming of standing beside a flowing stream is a symbol of the continuance of life. It could also be interpreted either as an encouragement to 'go with the flow' of events or a warning not to let opportunities pass one by. The meaning should be clear within the context of the dream and the circumstances to be found in waking life.

Watching as vital water drains away through cracks in arid land or a broken container is to become aware of the passing of time and the mourning of lost opportunities. To dream of drawing water from a well reflects the desire to draw on the sustaining resources of the self, specifically the knowledge and wisdom gained from our past experiences.

Secluded lakes feature in many myths and legends because of their mystical significance as places of initiation and because of the belief that they were openings between the earth and the underworld. Dreams of bathing under a waterfall in a secluded clearing could be interpreted as the need to cleanse oneself of worldly concerns and perhaps to embrace a more

positive, less materialistic way of life. At a deeper level such dreams might be first signs of a spiritual awakening and a growing awareness of a greater reality.

## FIRE

Dreams featuring fire are usually of a destructive and disturbing nature with the dreamer fleeing uncontrollable flames as his or her house burns to the ground. Fire can also be seen as a purifying force, as its over-use in the climax of many cheap horror movies has shown. If fire reduces your dream-house to ashes, interpret it as an exorcism of some out-moded ideas and attitudes or as a rather heavy-handed hint that it is time to move on!

In the dreamscape fire is also a symbol of the light of knowledge and awareness illuminating the darkness of ignorance. If you find yourself searching through a strangely familiar house in the dark with only a torch to light your way, it is likely that you are looking to discover previously hidden aspects of your personality, specifically the aptly named 'shadow self'. Alternatively, you might finally be looking to shed light on long-neglected memories as symbolized by the cobwebbed recesses of the rooms. Careful consideration of the symbolic significance of the decor and style of the room, the furniture and the objects which you find will be needed to reveal the true

meaning of the dream.

As a symbol of the hearth at the heart of the house, a dream of fire can be recalling the emotional warmth and security of the family home. Such a dream may also symbolize the flaring up of passions to comfort, scar or consume both lover and beloved. The size and intensity of the fire should give further clues as to which of these situations is apt.

A bonfire can be a very revealing image if you can recall who lit it and who is represented by the dummy, or 'Guy', which is invariably to be found on top of the pile!

Fire and water are traditionally thought to be mutually exclusive, with water extinguishing fire and fire transforming water to steam, symbolizing conflict or dying passion. However, in the dreamscape, if flames are reflected in water the dream is drawing the attention to the idea that the active male aspect of the dreamer and his or her passive feminine aspect are balanced and should be considered as complementary.

## MOON

The moon is a primary symbol of the mutable feminine principle and also of the mysteries of the night. From ancient times the moon has been the muse of our dreams, presiding over the hours of sleep. Its appearance in the dreamscape hints at the mysterious and intuitive aspects

of the personality and also marks the waxing and waning of the unconscious.

For a man to dream of the full moon is often symbolic of his awakening anima or feminine nature, although it can also refer to his mother, partner or sister.

For a woman such a dream can symbolize a mother, sister or close female friend, but is more likely to refer to an intensifying sensitivity or developing intuition. There is also evidence to suggest that many women dream of the moon after conception but before their pregnancy has been confirmed by a doctor.

If, as is common, the moon is seen reflected in water the dream's main theme is the emotions, most likely a reference to a woman's indifference towards a partner, family member or friend, for the moon is traditionally considered to be 'cold'. Alternatively, it could be signifying that we are under the spell of someone who has power over our emotions and that we may be deceiving ourselves into believing that they care for us. But if the moon appears as a luminous one-dimensional shape rather than as a realistic, planetary body, it is being used as a symbolic cliché for an idealized romance. Perhaps the lover is a composite of all the qualities we desire in a partner, or represents someone who is unattainable in waking life.

The lunar cycles are symbolic

of the stages of life on earth with the three-day phase, known as the 'dark side of the moon', seen as a symbol of transition.

The moon also mirrors the psychological condition, with the dark side of the moon being synonymous with the unconscious and insanity (hence the term 'lunacy'). For this reason – and the fact that for centuries the night was widely considered to be the time when evil walked abroad – the moon has sinister associations which the dream may be drawing upon. However, a full, radiant moon seen in a peaceful star-studded sky signifies wholeness and serenity. The precise meaning of such an ambiguous symbol can only be determined by an examination of the context of the dream.

## SUN

The sun is the primary symbol of the active masculine principle and of the source of life. As such it has been an image for heightened awareness, wisdom and spiritual illumination since ancient times. For a woman to dream of the sun is often symbolic of her awakening animus or masculine qualities, although the image can also refer to her father, a brother, son or male partner. For a man the sun can symbolize his father, a brother or close male friend, but is more likely to reflect a growing understanding of the world and the fulfilment of his paternal instincts. To dream of the rising sun is a sign that a new phase of your life is beginning or of the birth of new ideas (hence the expression 'it dawned on me to try something else'). Such a dream can also be a reminder to someone who is depressed that no matter how bleak the present situation might appear, the source of life is ever present and that a 'new day will dawn' with new opportunities.

To see the setting sun is to accept that a phase of your life is over. To dream of the sun reflecting in water suggests that you have achieved a balance between the forces of action and emotion in yourself, or that at an unconscious level you have accepted a female partner (symbolized by the water) as reflecting your light without extinguishing your energy. To see the sun partly obscured by clouds is symbolic of temporary difficulties, but hints at the dreamer's ability to look beyond them and imagine a successful outcome. But the sun also has its negative aspect. Dreaming of a sun-scorched garden is likely to be reminding the man who prides himself on being practical and physical that all growing things need water (that is, nurturing the emotions) and a spell in the shade (that is, rest) if they are to thrive and grow straight (that is, balanced). Be aware, too, that in dreams the sun can illuminate the darkest corners of the unconscious, although it will only do this in order to help us fully understand ourselves.

## STREETS, PATHS, TRACKS

Streets and paths usually symbolize the dreamer's journey through life in general. In some cases, however, the path can relate to a current situation. Straight, smooth, well-defined paths indicate that we know where we are going and how to get there with the minimum of distractions and effort. Winding paths can suggest that we are anticipating problems which might not exist and would rather explore all the options than go straight to our goal, even if this means delay.

Tracks and paths through dense woodland or forest indicate unknown difficulties ahead. Our attitude to entering the wood should indicate our attitude to life and those events.

The presence of steep, rocky and indistinct paths suggest that we view life mostly as a lonely, uphill struggle and that we have little idea of commitment or of our overall direction.

If we are presented with a choice of several paths, it is clear that the time has come for a decision in waking life. Even if there are no obvious choices to be made, such dreams could be encouraging us to take up a new challenge rather than stagnate in our present, albeit safe, situation.

# Index

## Acknowledgements

Executive Editor Jane McIntosh

Senior Editor Rachel Lawrence

Executive Art Editor Rozelle Bentheim

Designer Nigel Soper

Picture Research Vickie Walters

Senior Production Controller Manjit Sihra

## Picture Acknowledgements

AKG, 6 ©ADAGP, Paris and DACS, London
    2005, 14, 24 top

Getty Images Chris Cheadle 8/Ferguson &
    Katzman 23, Jeff Spielman 25, 40, 56,76,1

Octopus Publishing Group Limited 45, 51, 59,
    62, 66, 68, 73, 77, 79, 82, 83, 87, 90, 95,
    106, 112, 117, 122

Rubberball Productions 32, 33, 37, 38, 50, 53,
    57 bottom, 88, 91, 100, 113

Science Photo Library/Latin Stock 17 top

TopFoto/The Charles Walker Collection 20 top